LINUX
ADMINISTRATION

The Ultimate Beginners Guide to Learn Linux Step by Step

David A. Williams

© Copyright 2019 - All rights reserved.

The content contained within this book may not be reproduced, duplicated or transmitted without direct written permission from the author or the publisher.

Under no circumstances will any blame or legal responsibility be held against the publisher, or author, for any damages, reparation, or monetary loss due to the information contained within this book. Either directly or indirectly.

Legal Notice:

This book is copyright protected. This book is only for personal use. You cannot amend, distribute, sell, use, quote or paraphrase any part, or the content within this book, without the consent of the author or publisher.

Disclaimer Notice:

Please note the information contained within this document is for educational and entertainment purposes only. All effort has been executed to present accurate, up to date, and reliable, complete information. No warranties of any kind are declared or implied. Readers acknowledge that the author is not engaging in the rendering of legal, financial, medical or professional advice. The content within this book has been derived from various sources. Please consult a licensed professional before attempting any techniques outlined in this book.

By reading this document, the reader agrees that under no circumstances is the author responsible for any losses, direct or indirect, which are incurred as a result of the use of information contained within this document, including, but not limited to, — errors, omissions, or inaccuracies.

TABLE OF CONTENTS

INTRODUCTION 1

CHAPTER 1: INSTALLING RED HAT ENTERPRISE LINUX ON YOUR COMPUTER 4

Creating Red Hat Enterprise Linux 7 Installation Media on Windows 5

Creating Red Hat Enterprise Linux 7 Installation Media on Mac OS X 7

Installing Red Hat Enterprise Linux 7 9

CHAPTER 2: THE LINUX COMMAND LINE 13

The Bash Shell 13

Basics of Shell 15

Executing Commands on the Bash Shell 16

Shortcuts to Edit the Command Line 20

Managing Files using Commands on the Command Line 21

Directory Creation 29

Deleting Files and Directories 31

File Globbing 32

CHAPTER 3: MANAGING TEXT FILES 35

Redirecting the Output from a File to another File or Program ... 35

Rearranging the Existing Content in Vim 45

Using the Graphical Editor to Edit Text Files in Red Hat Enterprise Linux 7 46

CHAPTER 4: USER AND GROUP MANAGEMENT 49

Users and Groups 49

Primary Group: 51

Supplementary Group: 52

Getting Superuser Access 52

Using Su to Switch Users 53

Managing User Accounts 55

User Password Management 60

Access Restriction 63

CHAPTER 5: ACCESSING FILES IN LINUX AND FILE SYSTEM PERMISSIONS 65

Linux File System Permissions 65

Managing File System Permissions using the Command Line 68

CHAPTER 6: LINUX PROCESS MANAGEMENT 76

Processes 76

Controlling Jobs 81

Running Background Jobs 82

Killing Processes 84

Process Monitoring 92

CHAPTER 7: SERVICES AND DAEMONS IN LINUX 99

Identifying System Processes Started Automatically 99

Service states 102

Enabling System Daemons to Start or Stop at Boot 106

CHAPTER 8: OPENSSH SERVICE **108**
　Using SSH to Access the Remote Command Line 108
　SSH Based Authentication 111
　Customizing the SSH Configuration 112

CHAPTER 9: LOG ANALYSIS **115**
　Architecture of System Logs 115
　Syslog File Review 117
　Reviewing Journal Entries for Systemd 120
　Systemd Journal Preservation 122
　Maintaining time accuracy 124
　The Chronyd Service 126

CHAPTER 10: ARCHIVING FILES **128**
　Managing Compressed Archives 128

CONCLUSION **132**

Introduction

The term Linux refers to a kernel or an operating system that was developed by Linus Torvals along with a few other contributors. The first time it was released publicly in September 1991. In a world where Microsoft was charging consumers for an operating system like Windows, the advantage of Linux was that it was an open-source software meaning that programmers had the option to customize it, create their own operating system out of it and use it as per their requirement. The Linux operating system code was written mostly in the C programming language.

There are literally hundreds of operating systems available today, which use the Linux kernel and the most popular among them are Ubuntu, Debian, Fedora and Knoppix. This is not the end of the list as new operating systems come up almost every year, which use the kernel from the original Linux system.

Linux was a milestone in computing and technology and most of the mobile phones, web servers, personal computers, cloud-servers, and supercomputers today are powered by Linux. The job profile of Linux System Administration refers to that of maintaining operations on a Linux based system and ensuring maximum uptime from the system, in short, making sure that the system is consumed in the most optimum possible way. In the modern world, most of your devices run on a Linux powered server or are associated with a Linux system in some way or the other because of its high stability and open source nature.

Owing to this, the job a Linux Administrator revolves around the following.

- Linux File System
- Managing the superuser on the Linux system known as Root
- Command Line using the Bash Shell
- Managing users, file and directories

You can think of it as maintaining your own personal computer, which you would do at home, but on a larger scale, in this case for an entire organization. Linux system administration is a critical requirement for organizations in the modern world and, therefore, there is a huge demand in the market for this profile. The job description may vary from one organization to another, but the fundamentals of Linux Administration remain the same for every organization. The following responsibilities are associated with the profile of a system administrator.

- Maintaining regular backups of the data of all users on the system.

- Analyzing logs for errors to continuously improve the system.

- Maintain and enhance the existing tools for users of the system and for the Linux environment.

- Detecting problems and solving them, which range from user login issues to disaster recovery.

- Troubleshoot other problems on the system.

Perhaps, the most important skill to be found in a system admin is performing under a lot of load and stress. A system admin usually works a seven day week wherein he or she is on call two days a week and has to come online as soon as there is an issue with the system and must be quick to resolve it so that the system goes online immediately. A system or a server, if kept down for a long time can lead to losses worth thousands of dollars for an organization. As an example, take the website of the shopping giant Amazon. If the Amazon website went down even for one hour, all sales would suffer, leading to huge losses in revenue. This is where a system admin steps in and saves the day. The role of a system admin is nothing short of a superhero who saves an organization whenever the need arises.

CHAPTER 1

Installing Red Hat Enterprise Linux on your Computer

In this chapter, we will learn how to install Red Hat Enterprise Linux 7 on your computer. It is advisable to have a Linux operating system installed before you begin with all the other chapters as doing activities mentioned in the upcoming chapters will only give you hands on experience on a Linux system, which will help you understand Linux Administration better.

We will first need to create installation media to install Red Hat Enterprise Linux 7 on your computer. Depending on whether your current computer has Windows as an operating system or Mac OS X as an operating system, the steps to create the installation media for Red Hat Enterprise Linux 7 will differ. Let us go through the steps to create installation media on both Windows and Mac OS X one by one.

Before creating the installation media, you will need to download a Red Hat Enterprise Linux 7 installation image, which you will later load onto the installation media. You can download the installation ISO from for Red Hat Enterprise Linux 7 from the following URL.

https://developers.redhat.com/products/rhel/download

Make sure that you download from the link that says DVD ISO as that is the image that contains the complete installation for Red Hat Enterprise Linux 7.

Note: You will need to register on the website before you can download the Red Hat Enterprise Linux 7 installation ISO. You can do this when you are prompted to create an account to download the ISO.

Once you have downloaded the ISO required for installation, you can proceed with creating the installation media. Installation media can be a DVD, SD card or a USB drive. The following steps will help you create installation media on a USB drive on Windows and Mac OS X.

Creating Red Hat Enterprise Linux 7 Installation Media on Windows

The process of creating installation media for Red Hat Enterprise Linux 7 on a Windows machine is simple and straightforward. There are many tools available on the Internet using, which you can create the installation media by writing the Red Hat Enterprise Linux 7 ISO image to the USB drive. We have tested many tools and we recommend that you create the installation media using a tool called Fedora Media Writer. It can be downloaded from the following URL.

https://github.com/FedoraQt/MediaWriter/releases

You can download the .EXE file available on this GitHub repository to install it on your Windows machine. You can then proceed with the steps given below to complete the creation of installation media for Red Hat Enterprise Linux 7.

1. Download Fedora Media Writer from

    https://github.com/FedoraQt/MediaWriter/releases

    Make sure that you download from the link that says DVD ISO as that is the image that contains the complete installation for Red Hat Enterprise Linux 7

2. By this time you would have already downloaded the ISO for Red Hat Enterprise Linux 7 from their website as mentioned earlier. If not, you can download it from https://developers.redhat.com/products/rhel/download

3. Plug the USB drive into your computer, which you intend to use as the bootable media for installing Red Hat Enterprise Linux 7

4. Launch Fedora Media Writer

5. When the main window pops up, click on Custom Image and then navigate to the path where you have downloaded the Red Hat Enterprise Linux 7 ISO and select it

6. You will see a drop-down menu, which lets you select the drive on, which you want to write the ISO. You should be able to see the USB drive that you have plugged in. Select the USB drive

7. If your USB drive is not available in the drop-down, plug it out and plug it in again and launch Fedora Media Write again

8. Click on Write To Disk, which will initiate the media creation. Kindly ensure that the USB drive is plugged in until the process is complete. The installation media creation time will depend on the size of the ISO image and the USB drive's write speed.

9. You will see a popup saying Complete when the media creation process is finished.

10. You can now click on the Safely Remove Hardware icon in the taskbar of your Windows computer and physically remove the USB drive.

And with that, you have successfully created installation media for Red Hat Enterprise Linux 7 on a USB drive using your Windows machine.

Creating Red Hat Enterprise Linux 7 Installation Media on Mac OS X

The installation media for Red Hat Enterprise Linux 7 is created using the command line utility on Mac OS X. We will be using the *dd* command to create the installation media. The steps to create the installation media are as follow.

1. Download Fedora Media Writer from

    https://github.com/FedoraQt/MediaWriter/releases

    Make sure that you download from the link that says DVD ISO as that is the image that contains the complete installation for Red Hat Enterprise Linux 7

2. By this time you would have already downloaded the ISO for Red Hat Enterprise Linux 7 from their website as mentioned

earlier. If not, you can download it from https://developers.redhat.com/products/rhel/download

3. Plug the USB drive into your computer, which you intend to use as the bootable media for installing Red Hat Enterprise Linux 7

4. Launch the terminal

5. First, we need to identify the path for the USB drive using the *diskutil list* command. The path of the device will have a format, which will be like */dev/disknumber* where *number* denotes the number of the disk. In the example, we are using in the next step, the *disknumber* is *disk2*

6. You should see something listed like
   /dev/disk2

#:	Type	Name	Size	Identifier
0:	Windows_NTFS	SanDisk USB	8.0 GB	disk2s1

   You can identify your USB drive by comparing the type, name and size columns, which should give you a fair idea if it is the USB drive you plugged in or not.

7. To make sure that you have the correct device name for your USB drive, you can unmount the USB drive by using the command *diskutil* */dev/disknumber*. Note that you will be prompted with an error message that states **failed to unmount** if you try to unmount a system drive.

8. The *dd* command of the Linux terminal can be used to start writing the image to the USB drive.
   $ sudo dd if=/pathtoISO of=/dev/rdisknumber bs=1m>

   We are using *rdisknumber* instead of just *disknumber* because it is a faster method to write the ISO to the USB drive.

Note that you will need to replace the *pathtoISO* part with the actual path of the downloaded Red Hat Enterprise Linux 7 ISO on your Mac OS X machine.

9. This will now begin the writing process. You will need to wait until the writing completes, as you will not see anything until the process actually completes.

   The status of the writing progress can be displayed on the terminal by sending the Ctrl+t input from your keyboard.

   load: 2.01 cmd: dd 3675 uninterruptible 0.00u 1.92s

   114+0 records in

   114+0 records out

   116451517 bytes transferred in 125.843451 secs (1015426 bytes/sec)

10. The installation media creation time will depend on the size of the ISO image and the USB drive's write speed.

11. Once the transfer of data is complete, the USB drive can be unplugged.

This is it. You have successfully created installation media for Red Hat Enterprise Linux 7 on a USB drive using your Mac OS X machine.

Installing Red Hat Enterprise Linux 7

There are various options for installing Red Hat Enterprise Linux 7 but the steps we have provided in this section will help you install Red Hat Enterprise Linux 7 with minimal software and no graphical interface. You do not need to panic because of the absence of a graphical interface as most tasks that need to be performed as a Linux System Administrator are done using the command line.

Let us begin with the Red Hat Enterprise Linux 7 installation using the USB media drive that you have created in the previous section.

1. Plug in the USB drive into your computer's USB port and start your computer. You should make sure that you have enabled USB boot in your computer's BIOS settings

2. Once the computer boots up, you should be able to see a list of bootable devices and one of them would be your USB drive titled Red Hat Enterprise Linux 7

3. Once the system is up, you will get an option to choose your language. Click on Continue after you have selected the required language

4. You will now be presented with the Installation Summary screen where you can customize the installation of Red Hat Enterprise Linux 7 as per your needs. Select the Date and Time to configure the locale for your system using the world map that is provided and then click on Done

5. On the next screen, choose the language for your system and for your keyboard. We would recommend that you use the English language

6. The installation source for your Red Hat Enterprise Linux 7 will be the USB drive primarily, but you can add other sources for the repositories by specifying locations on the Internet on your local network using protocols such as FTP, HTTP, HTTPS, etc. Once you have defined all your sources, click on Done. You can just leave it on the default source if you do not have any other sources to be used

7. Now, you can select the software that has to be installed along with the operating system. As we have discussed, we will only be installing software that is essential. To do this, select on Minimal Install along with Compatibility Libraries Add-ons and click on Done

8. On the next step, we will configure partitions for the system. Click Installation Destination and then choose LVM scheme for partition, which will give optimized management for the disk space and then click on "Click here to create them automatically"

9. You will be presented with the default partition scheme, which you can edit as per your requirements. As we are going to use the Red Hat Enterprise Linux 7 operating system to learn server administration, you can use the essential partition scheme as given below

   /boot partition, which should have disk space of 500 MB and should be a non-LVM partition
   /root partition with a minimum disk space of 20 GB and an LVM partition
   /home partition, which should be an LVM partition
   /var partition with a minimum disk space of 20 GB and an LVM partition

   The filesystem that you need to use is XFS, which is the world's most advanced filesystem right now. Once you have specified the edits for the partitions, click on Update Settings and then click Done followed by Accept Changes, which will apply your edits to the system.

10. This is the final step before initiating the Red Hat Enterprise Linux 7 installation. You need to setup the network. Select Network and Hostname, which will allow you to specify a hostname for your system. You can use a short hostname for the system or use a Fully Qualified Domain Name (FQDN)

11. Once you have specified the network, you can toggle the Ethernet button on top to ON to switch on the network. If you have a router, which has a DHCP that allots IPs to devices, your IP will now be visible. If not, you can click on the Configure button to manually specify the settings for your network

12. Once you have configured the Ethernet settings, click on Done and you will be presented with the Installation screen. You will get one last chance to review your installation settings before the setup starts writing files to your disk. After reviewing, click on the Begin Installation option to start the installation.

13. The installation will now start writing files to your hard disk. Meanwhile, you will be prompted to create a new user for your system along with a password. Click on Root Password and supply a password that is strong and has at least 8 characters with a combination of the alphabet and numbers. Click on Done

14. Next, you can create a new user other than root and provide the credentials for this user. We recommend that you make this new user a system administrator who will have privileges similar to root user by using the *sudo* command. So check the box, which says "Make this user administrator" and then click Done. Give the installation some time to complete

15. Once the installation is complete, you will see a message confirming the same and that you can now reboot the system and get ready to use it

Voila! You can now unplug your installation media, which is the USB drive and restart your computer. You will be presented with the login screen for a minimal installation of Red Hat Enterprise Linux 7. You can either use the root user or the additional user that you created to login into the system.

CHAPTER 2

The Linux Command Line

In this chapter, we will learn about the Linux Command Line and how to use it to perform various tasks on your Linux operating system. By the end of this chapter, you will be well versed with the basic commands that are used on the command line and also commands that are used to manage files and folders on a Linux system.

The Bash Shell

The command line utility available on Linux operating systems is known as BASH, which is short for Bourne-Again Shell. The command line utility is basically an interface, which allows you to give instructions in text-mode to the computer and its operating system. There are different types of shell interfaces that are available in the many Unix0-ike systems that have been developed over the years, but Red Hat Enterprise Linux 7 uses the bash shell. The bash shell is an evolved and improved version of the former popular shell known as Bourne Shell.

The bash shell displays a string, which implies that it is waiting for a command to be input by the user. This string that you see is called the shell prompt. For a user that is not a root user, the shell prompt ends with a $ symbol.

[student@desktop ~]$

If the root user is logged into the system, the shell prompt ends with a # symbol. The change in this symbol quickly lets the user know if he is logged in as root or a regular user so that mistakes and accidents can be avoided.

[root@desktop ~]#

If you need an easy comparison, the bash shell in Linux operating systems is similar to the command prompt utility that is available in Windows operating systems, nut you can say that the scripting language used in bash is far more sophisticated compared to the scripting that can be done in command prompt. Bash is also comparable to the power shell utility, which was made available from Windows 7 and Windows Server 2008 R2. The bash shell has been called as a very powerful tool for administration by many professionals. You can automate a lot of tasks on your Linux system using the scripting language that is provided by the bash shell. Additionally, the bash shell also has the option to perform many other tasks, which are complicated or even impossible if tried via a graphical interface.

The bash shell is accessed through a tool known as the terminal. The input to the terminal is your keyboard and the output device is your display monitor. Linux operating systems also provide something known as virtual consoles, which can be used to access the bash shell as well. So, you will have multiple virtual consoles on the base physical console and each virtual console can act as a separate terminal. Also, you can use each virtual console to create login sessions for different users.

Basics of Shell

There are three parts to commands that are entered on the shell prompt.

1. *Command* that you want to run
2. *Options* that will define the behavior of the command
3. *Arguments, which* are the command's targets

The command basically defines that program that you want to execute. The options that follow the command can be none, one or more. The options govern the behavior of the command and define what the command will do. Options are usually used with one dash or two dashes. This is done so that we can differentiate options from arguments. Example: -a or --all

Arguments also follow the command on the command line and can be one or more like options. Arguments indicate the target on, which a command is supposed to operate.

Let us take an example command

usermod -L John

The command in this example is *usermod*

The option is *-L*

The argument is *John*

What this command does is locks the password of the user John on the system.

To be effective with the commands on the command line, it is essential for a user to know what options can be used with a particular command. If you run the *--help* option with any command, you will get a set of options, which can be passed with that particular command. So, it's not really necessary that you know all the options that are to be used by all the commands by heart. The list will also tell you what each option does.

The use of statements can sometimes seem very difficult and complicated to read. Once you get used to certain conventions, reading the statement becomes much easier.

- Options are surrounded by square brackets [ ]
- If a command is followed by ... it specifies the arbitrary length list of items belonging to that type
- If there are multiple items and if the pipe separates them | it implies that you can specify only one of them
- Variables are represented using text, which is in angle brackets <>. So if you see <filename>, you have to replace it with the filename that you wish to pass

For example, check the below command

[student@desktop ~]$ date --help

date [OPTION]... [+FORMAT]

This indicates that the command date takes the options represented by [OPTION]... with another option [FORMAT], which will be prefixed with the + symbol.

Executing Commands on the Bash Shell

The Bourne Again Shell, known as bash, does the job of interpreting commands that are input by the user on the shell prompt. We have already learned how the string that you type in at shell prompt is divided into three parts, command, options and arguments. Every word that you type into the shell is separated using blank space. The program that is already installed on the system is defined by every command that you type, and every command has options and arguments that are associated with it.

When you have typed a command on the shell prompt along with the options and arguments and are ready to run it, you can press the Enter key on the keyboard, which will execute that command. You will then see the output of that command displayed on the terminal and when the output completes, you will be presented with the shell prompt again, which is an indication that the previous command has been executed successfully. If you wish to type more than one command on a single line, you can use a semicolon to separate the commands.

Let us go through some simple commands that are used on a daily routine on the command line in Red Hat Enterprise Linux 7 and other Linux based operating systems.

The *date* command will display the current date and time of the system. You can also use this command to set the time of the system. If you are passing an argument with the + sign for the date command, it indicates the format in, which you want the date to be displayed on the output.

[student@desktop ~]$ date

Sat Aug 5 08:15:30 GMT 2019

[student@desktop ~]$ date +%R

08:15

[student@desktop ~]$ date +%x

08/05/2019

The *passwd* command can be used to change the password of a user. You will, however, need to specify the original password for the given user before you can set a new password. The command requires you to specify a strong password, which makes it necessary to include letter belonging to lowercase and uppercase, numbers, and symbols. You also need to ensure that the password being specified is not a word in the dictionary. The root user has the option to change the password of any other user on the system.

[student@desktop ~]$ passwd

Changing password for user student.

Changing password for student.

(current) UNIX password: type old password here

New password: Specify new password here

Retype new password: Type new password again

passwd: all authentication tokens updated successfully.

File types and extensions are not specified in a Linux operating system. The *file* command can scan any file and tell you the kind of file it is. The file you want to classify needs to be passed as an argument to the file command.

[student@desktop ~]$ file /etc/passwd

/etc/passwd: ASCII text

If you are passing a folder/directory as an argument to the file command, it will tell you that it is a directory.

[student@desktop ~]$ file /home

/home: directory

The next set of commands are ***head*** and ***tail**, which* print the first ten lines and the last ten lines of a file respectively. Both these commands can be combined with the option *-n, which* can be used to specify the number of lines that you want to be displayed.

[student@desktop ~]$ head /etc/passwd

This will print the first 10 lines that are there in the passwd file.

[student@desktop ~]$ tail - n /etc/passwd

This will print the last 3 lines that are there in the passwd file.

The ***wc*** command is used to count lines, words and characters in a file that is passed as an argument. It supports options such as -l, -w, -c, which stands for lines, words, and characters respectively.

[student@desktop ~]$ wc /etc/passwd

30   75   2009 /etc/passwd

This shows that there are 30 lines, 75 words and 2009 characters in the file passwd.

If you pass the -l, -c, -w options along with the wc command, it will only display the count of lines, words or characters based on, which option you have passed.

The ***history*** command displays all the commands that you have typed previously along with the command number. You can use the ! mark along with the command number to expand what was typed in that command along with the output.

[student@desktop ~]$ history

1 clear

2 who

3 pwd

[student@desktop ~]$!3

/home/student

This shows that we used !3 to expand the pwd command, which shows the present working directory for, which the output was /home/student, which was the home directory of the student user.

You can use the arrow keys to navigate through the output given by the history command. Up Arrow will take you to the commands on top and Down Arrow will take you to the commands below. Using the Right Arrow and the Left Arrow keys, you can move on the current command and edit it.

Shortcuts to Edit the Command Line

There is an editing feature available on the command line in bash when you are interacting with bash. This helps you to move around the current command that you are typing so that you can make edits. We have already seen how we can use the arrow keys with the history command to move through commands. The following list will help you use edits when you are working on a particular command.

- **Ctrl+a**   This will take your cursor to the start of the command line
- **Ctrl+e**   This will take your cursor to the end of the command line
- **Ctrl+u**   Clear the line from where the cursor is to the start of the command line
- **Ctrl+k**   Clear the line from where the cursor is to the end of the command line

Ctrl+Left Arrow	Take the cursor to the start of the previous word
Ctrl+Right Arrow	Take the cursor to the start of the next word
Ctrl+r	Search for patterns in the history list of commands used

Managing Files using Commands on the Command Line

In this section, we will learn to execute commands that are needed to manage files and directories in Linux. You will learn how to move, copy, create, delete and organize files and directories using commands on the bash shell prompt.

Linux File System Hierarchy

Let us first understand the hierarchy of the file system in a Linux operating system. The Linux file system has a tree, which has directories forming the file system hierarchy. However, this is an inverted tree as the root starts from the top of the hierarchy in Linux and then the branches, which are directories and subdirectories extend below the root.

The root directory denoted by / sits at the top of the file system hierarchy. Although the root is denoted by / do note that the slash character / is also used to separate directories and filenames. As an example, take etc, which is a subdirectory of the root and is denoted by /etc. Similarly, if there is a file named logs in the /etc directory, we will reference it as /etc/logs

The subdirectories of root / are standard and store files based on their specific purpose. For example, files under /boot will contain files, which are needed to execute the boot process of the Linux operating system.

We will now go through the important directories in the Red Hat Enterprise Linux 7 file system hierarchy.

/usr

The shared libraries, which are installed with the software, are stored in this directory. It has subdirectories further, which are important such as

/usr/bin: User command files

/usr/sbin: Commands used in system administration

/usr/local: Files of software that has been customized locally

/etc

System configuration files are stored here.

/var

Files that change dynamically such as databases, log files, etc. are stored in this directory.

/run

This directory contains files that were created during runtime and were created since the last boot. The files created here get recreated on the next boot.

/home

This is the home directory for all users that are created on the system. The users get to store their personal data and configurations under their specific home path.

/root

> This is the home directory of the root user who is also the superuser of the system.

/tmp

> This is a directory used to store temporary files. Files, which are older than 10 days and have not been accessed or modified automatically get deleted. There is another directory at /var/tmp where file not accessed or modified in 30 days get deleted automatically.

/boot

> The files required to start the boot process are stored here.

/dev

> Contains files, which reference to hardware devices on the system.

Let us now learn how we can locate and access files on the Linux file system. In this section, we will learn to use absolute file paths, change the directory in, which we are currently working and learn commands, which will help us to determine the location and contents of a directory.

Absolute Paths

An absolute path indicates a name that is fully qualified. It begins from the root at /, which is followed by each subdirectory that is traversed through until you reach a specific file. There is an absolute path defined for every file that exists on the Linux file system, which can be identified using a simple rule. If the first character of the path is / then it implies an absolute path name.

For example, system messages are logged in a file called messages. The absolute path name for the messages file is /var/log/messages

There are relative path names in place as well since absolute path names can sometimes become very long to type.

When you first login to the Linux system, you are automatically placed in the location of your home directory. There is an initial directory in place for system processes as well. After that, both users and system processes navigate through other directories based on their requirement. The current location of a user or a system process is known as a working directory or current working directory.

Relative Paths

A relative path refers to the unique path, which is required to reach a file but this path is only from the current directory that you are in and does not start with root /

The rule, as mentioned, is simple. If the path does not begin with a / symbol, it is a relative path for the file.

For example, if you are already working in the /var directory, then the relative path for the messages file for you will be log/messages

Navigating through paths

You can use the **pwd** command, which will output the path of the current working directory you are in. Once you know this information, you can use it to traverse to different directories using relative paths.

The **ls** command when used with a directory or directory path specifies the content of that particular directory. If you do not specify a directory with it, it will list the content of the directory that you are currently working in.

[student@desktop ~]$ pwd

/home/student

[student@desktop ~]$ ls

Documents   Music   Downloads   Pictures

You can use the **cd** command to change directories. For example, if you are in the directory /home/student and you want to go to the directory Music, you can use relative path to get there. However, if you would want to get into the Downloads directory, you will then need to use the absolute path.

[student@desktop ~]$ cd Music

[student@desktop Music]$ pwd

/home/student/Music

[student@desktop ~]$ cd /home/student/Downloads

[student@desktop Downloads]$ pwd

/home/student/Downloads

As you can see, the shell prompt will display the last part of the current directory that you are working in for convenience. If you are in /home/student/Music only Music is displayed at the shell prompt.

The **cd** command is used to navigate through directories. If you use cd with an argument of a relative path or an absolute path, your current working directory will switch to that path's end directory. You can also use **cd -,** **which** will take you back to the previous directory you were working in and if you use it again, you will be back to the directory that you switched from. If you just keep using it, you will keep alternating between two fixed directories.

The **touch** command is another simple command, which if applied to an existing file, updates its timestamp to the current timestamp without actually modifying the content of the file. If used by passing an argument for a filename that does not exist, it will create an empty file with that filename. This allows new users to touch and create files for practice since these files will not harm the system in any manner.

[student@desktop ~]$ touch Documents/test.txt

This will create an empty text file called test in the Documents subdirectory.

The **ls** command lists down the files and directories of the directory that you are in. If you pass the path of a directory with the ls command, it will list down the files and directories in that path.

The ls command can be used with options, which further help listing down files.

-l will list down all the files with timestamps and permissions of the files and directories. It will also list down the owner and the group of that file.

-a can be combined with -l to additionally list down hidden files and directories.

-R used with the above two options will list down files and directories recursively for all subdirectories.

When you list down the files and directories, you will see that the first two listing are a . and ..

. denotes the current directory and .. denotes the parent directory and these are present on the system in every directory.

File Management using Command Line

When we talk about file management, we are discussing how to create, delete, copy, and move files. The same set of actions can be performed on directories as well. It is very important to know your current working directory so that when you are managing files and directories, you know if you need to specify relative paths or absolute paths.

Let us go through a few commands that can be used for file management.

Activity	Single Source	Multiple Source
Copy file	cp file1 file2	cp file1 file2 file3 dir
Move file	mv file1 file2	mv file1 file2 file3 dir
Delete file	rm file1	rm -f file1 file2 file3
Create directory	mkdir dir	mkdir -p par1/par2/dir
Copy directory	cp -r dir1 dir2	cp -r dir1 dir2 dir3 dir4
Move directory	mv dir1 dir2	mv dir1 dir2 dir3 dir4
Delete directory	rm -r dir1	rm -rf dir1 dir2 dir3

mv file1 file2

The result of this is a rename

cp -r dir1 dir2

rm -r dir1

-r is used to process the source directory recursively

mv dir1 dir2

If dir2 exists, the content of dir1 will be moved to dir2. If it does not exist, dir1 will be renamed to dir2

cp file_1 file_2 file_3 directory

mv file_1 file_2 file_3 directory

cp -r directory1 directory2 directory3 directory4

mv directory1 directory2 directory3 directory4

Make sure that the last argument to be passed in the command should be a directory

rm -f file_1 file_2 file_3

rm -rf directory1 directory2 directory3

Kindly use this carefully as the -f uses a force option will delete everything without any confirmation prompt

mkdir -p par1/par2/dir

Kindly use this carefully as using -p will keep creating directories starting from the parent and irrespective of typing errors

Let us now go through these file management commands one by one to see how they work.

Directory Creation

You can use the **mkdir** command to create a directory, or even subdirectories. If a filename already exists or if the parent directory that you have specified does not exist, you will see errors generated. When you use the mkdir command along with the option **-p** it will create all parent directories along the path that do not exist. You need to be careful while using the -p option or you will end up creating directories that are not required, as it does not check for any spelling errors.

[student@desktop ~]$ mkdir Drawer

[student@desktop ~]$ ls

Drawer

As you can see, the new directory called Drawer is created in the home directory of the user.

[student@desktop ~]$ mkdir -p Thesis/Chapter1

[student@desktop ~]$ ls -R

Thesis   thesis_chapter1

As you can see, a new directory called Thesis was created and its subdirectory called Chapter1 was created at the same time.

Copy Files

The **cp** command is used to copy files. You can copy one or more files and syntax gives you the option to copy a file in the same directory or even copy a file in one directory to another file in another directory.

Note: The file that you are specifying at the destination should be a unique file. If you specify an existing file, you will end up overwriting the content of that existing file.

[student@desktop ~]$ cd Documents

[student@desktop Documents]$ cp one.txt two.txt

This will copy content of one.txt to two.txt

Similarly, you can copy from the current directory to a file in another directory as shown below.

[student@desktop ~]$ cp one.txt Documents/two.txt

This will copy content of one.txt in home directory to two.txt in the Documents sub-directory.

Move Files

The **mv** command can be used for two operations. If you are using it in the same directory, it will rename the file. If you are specifying another directory, it will move the file to the destination directory. The content of the files are retained if you rename or move the file. Also note that if the file size is huge, it may take longer to move from one directory to another.

[student@desktop ~]$ ls

Hello.txt

[student@desktop ~]$ mv Hello.txt Bye.txt

[student@desktop ~]$ ls

Bye.txt

You can see that in this example, since we were operating in the same directory, the mv command just renamed the Hello.txt file to Bye.txt

[student@desktop ~]$ ls

Hello.txt

[student@desktop ~]$ mv Hello.txt Documents

[student@desktop ~]$ ls Documents

Hello.txt

In this example, you will see that mv command moved Hello.txt file from the home directory to the Documents subdirectory.

Deleting Files and Directories

The **rm** command can be used to delete files. To delete directories, you will need to use **rm -r, which** will delete a directory, subdirectories and files in the whole path.

Note: There is nothing such as trash or recycle bin while operating from the command line. If you delete something, it is deleted permanently.

[student@desktop ~]$ ls

File1.txt Directory1

[student@desktop ~]$ rm file1

[student@desktop ~]$ ls

Directory1

[student@desktop ~]$rm -r Directory1

[student@desktop ~]$ ls

[student@desktop ~]$

The above command has demonstrated how you can delete a file and a directory using the rm command and using the -r option.

Also note that there is a **rmdir** command, which can be used to delete a directory as well provided that the directory is completely empty.

File Globbing

Management of files can become hectic if you are dealing with a large number of files. To overcome this hurdle, Linux offers a feature called file globbing, also known as path name expansion. It uses a technique called pattern matching, also known as wildcards, which is achieved with the use of meta-characters that expand and allow operations to be performed on multiple files at the same time.

*Pattern matching using * and ?*

[student@desktop ~]$ ls a*

alpha   apple

As you can see, the * is used as a wildcard to match a pattern, which has any files that begin with a.

You can try this pattern placing the start at different locations such as *a and *a*

[student@desktop ~]$ ls ???

are   tab   map

The number of question marks defines the number of characters in a file name. The output will show all files, which have a filename of 3 characters. You can try it with additional question marks as well.

Tilde Expansion

The tilde symbol ~ followed by a slash / will point to the active user's home directory. It can be followed by a directory name and can be used with commands such as cd and ls

[student@desktop ~]$ ls ~/Documents

file.txt hello.txt

[student@desktop ~]$ cd Documents

[student@desktop Documents]$

[student@desktop Documents]$ cd ~/

[student@desktop ~]$

Brace Expansion

The brace command is used when files have something in command, and you do not want to type it repetitively. It can be used with strings, which are comma-separated, and with expressions, which have a sequential nature. You can have nested braces as well.

[student@desktop ~]$ echo {sunday, monday, tuesday}.log

sunday.log   monday.log   tuesday.log

[student@desktop ~]$ echo file{1..3}.txt

file1.txt   file2.txt   file3.txt

[student@desktop ~]$echo file{a{1, 2}, b, c}.txt

filea1.txt   filea2.txt   fileb.txt   filec.txt

This is where we end this chapter and you have learned how to manage files and directories using simple commands using the command line interface on a Linux system. Most of these commands are generic to any flavor of a Linux operating system and not just Red Hat Enterprise Linux 7.

CHAPTER 3

Managing Text Files

In this chapter, we will learn how to create, view and edit text files on a Linux operating system. We will also learn how to redirect the output from one text file to another text file. We will learn to edit existing text files on the command shell prompt using a tool known as 'Vim'.

Redirecting the Output from a File to another File or Program

In this section, we will be discussing the terms such as standard input, standard output and standard error. We will further learn how to redirect outputs from a file to another file and redirect the output from a file to another program.

Standard Input, Standard Output, and Standard Error

When a program or a process is in running state, it will take inputs from somewhere and then write the output to a file or display it on the screen. When you are using a terminal on the Linux operating system, the input is usually taken from the keyboard and the output is sent to be displayed on the screen.

A process uses a number of channels known as file descriptors, which take some input and send some output. There are at least three file descriptors in every process.

1. Standard Input, also known as Channel 0, which takes inputs from the keyboard
2. Standard Output, also known as Channel 1, which sends outputs to the screen
3. Standard error, also known as Channel 3, which sends error messages

Let us go through the channel names for file descriptors

Number	Channel Name	Description	Default Connection	Usage
0	stdin	Standard input	Keyboard	Read only
1	stdout	Standard output	Terminal	Write only
2	stderror	Standard error	Terminal	Write only
3	filename	Other files	None	Read and/or Write

Redirecting Output to a File

The input/output redirection is used to replace default output destinations with file names or other devices. The output of a command, which usually is redirected to be displayed on the terminal screen, can be redirected to a file or a device or can even be discarded with the use of redirection.

When you redirect the standard output **stdout**, it will not appear as output on the terminal screen. This does not mean that error messages **stderr** will not appear on the screen if you only redirect standard output **stdout**. If you are redirecting the standard output to a file that does not exist, it will get created in the process. If the file already exists and you use a redirect that is not an append redirect, the existing file will be overwritten. Redirecting the standard output to /dev/null will discard all the output as it is redirected to an empty file.

Let us go through the output operators that are used for redirection.

>file

This will redirect the standard output stdout to the file and will overwrite any previous content in the file.

>>file

This will redirect the standard output stdout to the file and will append to any previous content in the file.

2>file

This will redirect the standard error stderr to the file and will overwrite any previous content in the file.

2>/dev/null

This will discard the standard error stderr by redirecting it to /dev/null

>file 2>&1

&>file

This will redirect the standard output stdout and standard error stderr to overwrite the same file

>>file 2>&1

&>>file

This will redirect the standard output stdout and standard error stderr to append to the same file

Note: The order of operator is very important as changing the order can lead to a complete change in the redirection.

For example, *>file 2>&1* will redirect the standard output stdout to the file and then redirect the standard error stderr to the same file.

If you were to change the order to *2>&1 >file* it will redirect the standard error to the default output place, which is the terminal screen and only redirect the standard output to the file.

Because of this confusion, many users prefer using the alternative operators *&>file* and *&>>file* for, which merge standard output and standard error and then redirect them to the file.

Let us quickly go through some example to understand output redirection better. There are many day to day system administration tasks that can be performed using the technique of output redirection.

1. Saving the timestamp in a file for future reference
   [student@desktop ~]$ date > ~/time

This will output the current timestamp and redirect it to the file named time in the student's home directory.

2. Copy the last 100 lines from a log file and save it in another file
   [student@desktop ~]$ tail -n 100 /var/log/messages > ~/logs
   This will copy the last hundred lines from the messages log file and save it in the logs file in the student's home directory.

3. Concatenation contents of 3 files into a single file
   [student@desktop ~]$ cat file1 file2 file3 > ~/onefile
   This will concatenate contents of file1, file2 and file3 and save it in a single file called onefile in the user's home directory.

4. List the hidden directories in the home directory and save the file names in a file
   [student@desktop ~]$ ls -a > ~/hiddenfiles
   This will list the hidden directories in the user's home directory and save the directory names in the file called hiddenfiles in the user's home directory.

5. Append the out of an echo command to an existing file
   [student@desktop ~]$ echo "Hello World" >> ~/file
   This will append the string Hello World to the file in the user's home directory.

6. Direct the standard output to one file and standard error to another file
   [student@desktop ~]$ find /etc -name passwd > ~/output 2> ~/error
   This will redirect the output to the output file and the errors to the error file in the student's home directory.

7. Discarding the error messages
   [student@desktop ~]$ find /etc -name passwd > ~/output 2>

/dev/null
   This will redirect the errors to /dev/null, which is an empty file and discard it.

8. Redirect standard output and standard error together in one file
   [student@desktop ~]$ find /etc -name passwd > &> ~/onefile
   This will redirect the standard output and standard error to the file onefile in the student's home directory.

Using the Pipeline

A pipeline is an operator, which separates one or more commands by using a pipe operator |

The pipe basically takes the standard output of the first command and passes it as standard input to the second command.

The output will keep passing through various commands, which are separated using the pipe and only the final output will be displayed on the terminal. We can visualize it as a flow of data through a pipeline from one process to another process and that data is being modified on its way by every command it passes through.

Let us go through some examples of the pipeline, which are useful in day to day tasks of system administration.

[student@desktop ~]$ ls -l /var/log | less

This will list the files and directories located at /var/log and display it on the terminal one screen at a time because of the less command.

[student@desktop ~]$ ls | wc –l

This command will pass the output through the pipe and the wc -l command will count the number of lines in the output and just display the number of lines and not the actual output of the ls command.

Pipelines, Redirections and the Tee command

As already discussed, when you are using the pipeline, the pipeline makes sure that all the data is processed and passed through every command and only the final output it displayed on the terminal screen. This means that if you were to use output redirection before a pipeline, the output would be redirected to the file and not to the next command in the pipeline.

[student@desktop ~]$ ls > ~/file | less

In this example, the output of the ls command was redirected to the file in the student's home directory and never passed to the less command and the final output never appeared on the terminal screen.

This is exactly where the **tee** command comes into the picture to help you work around such scenarios. If you are using a pipeline and use the tee command in it, tee will copy its standard input to standard output and at the same time will also redirect the standard output to the specified files named as arguments to the command. If you visualize data as water flowing through a pipe, tee command will be the T joint of that data, which will direct the output in two directions.

Let us go through some examples, which will help us understand how to use the tee command with pipelines.

[student@desktop ~]$ ls -l | tee ~/Documents/output | less

Using tee in this pipeline, firstly redirects the output of the ls command to the file at Documents/output in the student's home directory. After that, it also feeds the output of the ls command to the pipe as input to the less command, which is then displayed on the terminal screen.

[student@desktop ~]$ ls -l | less | tee ~/Documents/output

In this case, we see that tee is used at the end of the command. What this does is it displays the output of the commands in the pipeline on the terminal screen and saves the same output to the file at Documents/output in the student's home directory as well.

Note: You can redirect standard error while using the pipe, but you will not be able to use the merging operators &> and &>>

Therefore, if you wish to redirect both standard output and standard error while using the pipe, you will have to use it in the following manner.

[student@desktop ~]$ find -name / passwd 2>&1 | less

Using the Shell Prompt to Edit Text Files

In this section, we will learn how to use the shell prompt to create new files and edit existing files. We will also learn about Vim, which is a very popular editor used to edit files from the shell prompt.

Using Vim to edit files

One of the most interesting things about Linux is that it is designed and developed in a way where all information is stored in text-based files. There are two types of text files, which are used in linux. Flat files in, which text is stored in rows containing similar information, which you will find in the /etc directory, and Extensible Markup Language(XML) file, which have text stored using tags, which you will find in the /etc and /usr directories. The biggest advantage of text files is that they can be transferred from one system or platform to another without having the need to convert them, and they can also be viewed and edited using simple text editors.

Vim is a the most popular text editor across all Linux flavors and is an improved version of the previously popular vi editor. Vim can be configured as per the needs of a user and includes features like color formatting, split screen editing, and highlighting text for editing.

Vim works in 4 modes, which are used for different purposes.

1. Edit mode
2. Command mode
3. Visual edit mode
4. Extended command mode

When you first launch Vim, it will open in the command mode. The command mode is useful for navigation, cut and paste jobs, and other tasks related to manipulation of text. To enter the other modes of Vim, you need to enter single keystrokes, which are specific to every mode.

- If you use the i keystroke in the command mode, you will be taken to the insert mode, which lets you edit the text file. All content you type in the insert mode becomes a part of the file. You can return to the command mode by pressing the Esc key on the keyboard

- If you use the v keystroke in the command mode, you will be taken to the visual mode, where you can manipulate text by selecting multiple characters. You can use V and Ctrl+V to select multiple lines and multiple blocks, respectively. You can exit the visual mode by using the same keystroke that is v, V or Ctrl+V.

- The : keystroke takes you to the extended command mode, which lets you save the content that you typed to the file and exit the vim editor.

There are more keystrokes that are available in vim for advanced tasks related to text editing. Although it is known to be one of the best text editors in Linux in the world, it can get overwhelming for new users. We will go through the minimum keystrokes that are essential for anyone using vim to accomplish editing tasks in Linux.

Let us go through the steps given below to get some hands-on experience of vim for new users.

1. Open a file on the shell prompt using the command *vim filename.*

2. Repeat the text entry cycle given below as many times as possible until you get used to it.
   Use the arrow keys on the keyboard to position the cursor
   Press **i** to go to insert mode
   Enter some text of your choice
   You can use **u** to undo steps taken on the current line that you are editing
   Press the **Esc** key on the keyboard to return to the command mode

3. Repeat the following cycle, which teaches you to delete text, as many times as possible until you get the hang of it.
   Position the cursor using the arrow keys on the keyboard
   Delete a selection of text by pressing **x** on the keyboard
   You can use **u** to undo steps taken on the current line that you are editing

4. You can use the following keystrokes next to save, edit, write or discard the file.
   Enter **:w** to save/write the changes you have made to the file and stay in the command mode
   Enter **:wq** to save/write the changes to the file and exit Vim
   Enter **:q** to discard the changes that you have made to the file and exit Vim

Rearranging the Existing Content in Vim

The tasks of copy and paste are known as yank and put in Vim. This can be achieved using the keystrokes of **y** and **p**. To start, place the cursor at the first character where you wish to copy from and then enter the visual mode. You can now use the arrow keys to expand your selection. You can then press y to copy the text to the clipboard. Next place your cursor where you wish to paste the selected content and press **p**.

Let us go through the steps given below to understand how to use the copy and paste feature using yank and put in Vim.

1. Open a file on the shell prompt using the command *vim filename.*

2. Repeat the text selection cycle given below as many times as possible until you get used to it.
   Position your cursor to the first character using the arrow keys on the keyboard
   Enter the visual mode by pressing **v**
   Position your cursor to the last character using the arrow keys on the keyboard
   Copy the selection by using yank **y**
   Position your cursor to the location where you want to paste the content using the arrow keys on the keyboard
   Paste the selection by using put **p**

3. You can use the following keystrokes next to save, edit, write or discard the file.
   Enter **:w** to save/write the changes you have made to the file and stay in the command mode
   Enter **:wq** to save/write the changes to the file and exit Vim
   Enter **:q** to discard the changes that you have made to the file and exit Vim

Note: Before you take tips from the advanced vim users, it is advisable that you get used to the basics of vim as performing advanced functions in vim without proper knowledge may lead to modification of important files and result in permanent loss of information. You can learn more about the basics of vim by looking up the Internet for vim tips.

Using the Graphical Editor to Edit Text Files in Red Hat Enterprise Linux 7

In this section, we will learn to access, view and edit text files using a tool in Red Hat Enterprise Linux 7 known as **gedit**. We will also learn how to copy text between to or more graphical windows.

Red Hat Enterprise Linux 7 comes with a utility known as **gedit, which** is available in the graphical desktop environment of the operating system . You can launch gedit by following the steps given below.

Applications > Accessories > gedit

You can also launch gedit without navigating through the menu. You can press Alt+F2, which will open the Enter A Command dialog box. Type gedit in the text box and hit Enter.

Let us go through the basic keystrokes that are available in gedit. The menu in gedit will allow you to perform numerous tasks related to file management.

- Creating a new file: Navigate through File > New (Ctrl+n) on the menu bar or click the blank paper icon on the toolbar to start a new file

- Saving a file: Navigate through File > Save (Ctrl+s) on the menu bar or click the disk icon on the toolbar to save a file

- Open and existing file: Navigate through File > Open (Ctrl+o) on the menu bar or click on the Open icon on the toolbar. A window will open up showing you all the files on your system. Locate the file that you wish to open and select it and click on open

If you select multiple files and click on open, they will all open up and will have a separate tab under the menu bar. The tabs will display a filename for existing files or when you save a new file with a new name.

Let us now learn how to copy text between two or more graphical windows in Red Hat Enterprise Linux 7. Using the graphical environment in Red Hat Enterprise Linux 7, you can copy text between text windows, documents, and command windows. You can select the text that you want to duplicate using copy and paste, or you can move text using the cut and paste options. In either case, the text is stored in the clipboard memory so that you can paste it to a destination.

Let us go through the steps to perform these operations.

Selecting the text:

- Left click and hold the mouse button at the first character of the text

- Drag the mouse until you have selected all the desired content and then release the button. Make sure that you do not press any mouse button again as that will result in deselection of all the text

Pasting the selected text: There are multiple methods to achieve this. This is the first one.

- Right click the mouse on the selected text at any point
- A menu will be displayed, and you will get the option to either cut or copy
- Next, open the window where you want to paste the text and place the cursor in the desired location where you wish to paste the text. Right click the mouse again and select paste on the menu that appears

There is a shorter method to achieve the same result as well.

- Firstly, select the text that you need
- Go to the window where you wish to paste the text and place the cursor at the desired location in the window. Middle click the mouse just once and will paste the selected text

This method will help you copy and paste but not cut and paste. However, to emulate a cut and paste, you can delete the original text as it remains selected. The copied text remains in the clipboard memory and can be pasted again and again.

The last method is the one using shortcut keys on the keyboard:

- After selecting the text, you can press Ctrl+x to cut or Ctrl+c to copy
- Go to the window where you want to paste the text and place the cursor at the desired location
- Press Ctrl+v

CHAPTER 4

User and Group Management

In this chapter, we will learn about users and groups in Linux and how to manage them and administer password policies for these users. By the end of this chapter, you will be well versed with the role of users and groups on a Linux system and how they are interpreted by the operating system. You will learn to create, modify, lock and delete user and group accounts, which have been created locally. You will also learn how to manually lock accounts by enforcing a password-aging policy in the shadow password file.

Users and Groups

In this section, we will understand what users and groups are and what is their association with the operating system.

Who is a user?

Every process or a running program on the operating system runs as a user. The ownership of every file lies with a user in the system. A user restricts access to a file or a directory. Hence, if a process is running as a user, that user will determine the files and directories the process will have access to.

You can know about the currently logged-in user using the **id** command. If you pass another user as an argument to the id command, you can retrieve basic information of that other user as well.

If you want to know the user associated with a file or a directory, you can use the **ls -l** command and the third column in the output shows the username.

You can also view information related to a process by using the **ps** command. The default output to this command will show processes running only in the current shell. If you use the **ps a** option in the command, you will get to see all the process across the terminal. If you wish to know the user associated with a command, you can pass the **u** option with the ps command and the first column of the output will show the user.

The outputs that we have discussed will show the users by their name, but the system uses a user ID called UID to track the users internally. The usernames are mapped to numbers using a database in the system. There is a flat file stored at /etc/passwd, which stored the information of all users. There are seven fields for every user in this file.

username: password: UID: GID: GECOS: /home/dir: shell

username:

Username is simply the pointing of a user ID UID to a name so that humans can retain it better.

password:

This field is where passwords of users used to be saved in the past, but now they are stored in a different file located at /etc/shadow

UID:

It is a user ID, which is numeric and used to identify a user by the system at the most fundamental level

GID:

This is the primary group number of a user. We will discuss groups in a while

GECOS:

This is a field using arbitrary text, which usually is the full name of the user

/home/dir:

This is the location of the home directory of the user where the user has their personal data and other configuration files

shell:

This is the program that runs after the user logs in. For a regular user, this will mostly be the program that gives the user the command line prompt

What is a group?

Just like users, there are names and group ID GID numbers associated with a group. Local group information can be found at /etc/group

There are two types of groups. Primary and supplementary. Let's understand the features of each one by one.

Primary Group:

- There is exactly one primary group for every user

- The primary group of local users is defined by the fourth field in the /etc/passwd file where the group number GID is listed

- New files created by the user are owned by the primary group

- The primary group of a user by default has the same name as that of the user. This is a User Private Group (UPG) and the user is the only member of this group

Supplementary Group:

- A user can be a member of zero or more supplementary groups

- The primary group of local users is defined by the last field in the /etc/group file. For local groups, the membership of the user is identified by a comma separated list of user, which is located in the last field of the group's entry in /etc/group groupname: password:GID:list, of, users, in, this, group

- The concept of supplementary groups is in place so that users can be part of more group and in turn have to resources and services that belong to other groups in the system

Getting Superuser Access

In this section, we will learn about what the root user is and how you can be the root or superuser and gain full access over the system.

The root user

There is one user in every operating system that is known as the super user and has all access and rights on that system. In a Windows based operating system, you may have heard about the superuser known as the *administrator*. In Linux based operating systems, this superuser is known as the **root** user. The root user has the power to override any normal privileges on the file system and is generally used to administer and manage the system. If you want to perform tasks such as installing new software or removing an existing software, and other tasks such as manage files and directories in the system, a user will have to escalate privileges to the root user.

Most devices on an operating system can be controlled only by the root user, but there are a few exceptions. A normal user gets to control removable devices such as a USB drive. A non-root user can, therefore, manage and remove files on a removable device but if you want to make modifications to a fixed hard drive, that would only be possible for a root user.

But as we have heard, with great power comes great responsibility. Given the unlimited powers that the root user has, those powers can be used to damage the system as well. A root user can delete files and directories, remove or modify user accounts, create backdoors in the system, etc. Someone else can gain full control over the system if the root user account gets compromised. Therefore, it is always advisable that you login as a normal user and escalate privileges to the root user only when absolutely required.

As already mentioned, the root account on Linux operating system is the equivalent of the local Administrator account on Windows operating systems. It is a practice in Linux to login as a regular user and then use tools to gain certain privileges of the root account.

Using Su to Switch Users

You can switch to a different user account in Linux using the **su** command. If you do not pass a username as an argument to the su command, it is implied that you want to switch to the root user account. If you are invoking the command as a regular user, you will be prompted to enter the password of the account that you want to switch to. However, if you invoke the command as a root user, you will not need to enter the password of the account that you are switching to.

su - <username>

```
[student@desktop ~]$ su -
```

Passord: rootpassword

```
[root@desktop ~]#
```

If you use the command su username, it will start a session in a non-login shell. But if you use the command as su - username, there will be a login shell initiated for the user. This means that using su - username sets up a new and clean login for the new user whereas just using su username will retain all the current settings of the current shell. Mostly, to get the new user's default settings, administrators usually use the su - command.

sudo and the root

There is a very strict model implemented in linux operating systems for users. The root user has the power to do everything while the other users can do nothing that is related to the system. The common solution, which was followed in the past was to allow the normal user to become the root user using the su command for a temporary period until the required task was completed. This, however, has the disadvantage that a regular user literally would become the root user and gain all the powers of the root user. They could then make critical changes to the system like restarting the system and even delete an entire directory like /etc. Also, gaining access to become the root user would involve another issue that every user switching to the root user would need to know the password of the root user, which is not a very good idea.

This is where the **sudo** command comes into the picture. The sudo command lets a regular user run command as if they are the root user, or another user, as per the settings defined in the /etc/sudoers file. While other tools like su would require you to know the password of the root user, the sudo command requires you to know only your own password for authentication, and not the password of the account that you are trying to gain access to. By doing this, it allows the administrator of the system to allow a certain list of privileges to regular users such that they perform system administration tasks, without actually needing to know the root password.

Lets us see an example where the student user through sudo has been granted access to run the **usermod** command. With this access, the student user can now modify any other user account and lock that account

[student@desktop ~]$ sudo usermod -L username

[sudo] password for student: studentpassword

Another benefit of using the sudo access is that all commands that any user runs using sudo are logged to **/var/log/secure**.

Managing User Accounts

In this section, you will learn how to create, modify, lock and delete user accounts that are defined locally in the system. There are a lot of tools available on the command line, which can be invoked to manage local user accounts. Let us go through them one by one and understand what they do.

- ***useradd** username* is a command that creates a new user with the username that has been specified and creates default parameters for the user in the /etc/passwd file when the command is run without using an option. Although, the command will not set any default password for the new user and therefore, the user will not be able to login until a password has been set for them.

    The useradd --help will give you a list of options that can be specified for the useradd command and using these will override the default parameters of the user in the /etc/passwd file. For a few options, you can also use the **usermod** command to modify existing users.

There are certain parameters for the user, such as the password aging policy or the range of the UID numbers, which will be read from the /etc/login.defs file. The file only comes into picture while creating new users. Modifying this file will not make any changes to existing users on the system.

- *usermod --help* will display all the basic options that you can use with this command, which can be used to manage user accounts. Let us go through these in brief

-c, --comment COMMENT	This option is used to add a value such as full name to the GECOS field
-g, --gid GROUP	The primary group of the user can be specified using this option
-G, --groups GROUPS	Associate one or more supplementary groups with user
-a, --append	The option is used with the -G option to add the user to all specified supplementary groups without removing the user from other groups
-d, --home HOME_DIR	The option allows you to modify a new home directory for the user

-m, --move-home	You can move the location of the user's home directory to a new location by using the -d option
-s, --shell SHELL	The login shell of the user is changed using this option
-L, --lock	Lock a user account using this option
-U, --unlock	Unlock a user account using this option

- *userdel username* deletes the user from the /etc/passwd file but does not delete the home directory of that user. *userdel -r username* deletes the user from /etc/passwd and deletes their home directory along with its content as well.

- *id* displays the user details of the current user, which includes the UID of the user and group memberships. *id username* will display the details of the user specified, which includes the UID of the user and group memberships.

- *passwd username* is a command that can be used to set the user's initial password or modify the user's existing password.

  The root user has the power to set the password to any value. If the criteria for password strength is not met, a warning message will appear, but the root user can retype the same password and set the password for a given user anyway. If it is a regular user, they will need to select a password, which is at least 8 characters long, should not be the same as the username, or a previous word, or a word that can be found in the dictionary.

- **UID Ranges** are ranges that are reserved for specific purposes in Red Hat Enterprise Linux 7
  UID 0 is always assigned to the root user.
  UID 1-200 are assigned by the system to system processes in a static manner.
  UID 201-999 are assigned to the system process that does not own any file in the system. They are dynamically assigned whenever an installed software request for a process.
  UID 1000+ are assigned to regular users of the system.

Managing Group Accounts

In this section, we will learn about how to create, modify, and delete group accounts that have been created locally.

It is important that the group already exists before you can add users to a group. There are many tools available on the Linux command line that will help you to manage local groups. Let us go through these commands used for groups one by one.

- *groupadd groupname* is a command that if used without any options creates a new group and assigns the next available GID in the group range and defines the group in the /etc/login.defs file
  You can specify a GID by using the option **-g GID**

  [student@desktop ~]$ sudo groupadd -g 5000 ateam

  The **-r** option will create a group that is system specific and assign it a GID belonging to the system range, which is defined in the /etc/login.defs file.

  [student@desktop ~]$ sudo groupadd -r professors

- ***groupmod*** command is used to modify the parameters of an existing group such as changing the mapping of the groupname to the GID. The **-n** option is used to specify a new name to the group.

  [student@desktop ~]$ sudo groupmod -n professors lecturers

  The **-g** option is passed along with the command if you want to assign a new GID to the group.

[student@desktop ~]$ sudo groupmod -g 6000 ateam

- ***groupdel*** command is used to delete the group.

  [student@desktop ~]$ sudo groupdel ateam

  Using groupdel may not work on a group that is the primary group of a user. Just like userdel, you need to be careful with groupdel that you check that there are no files on the system owned by the user existing after deleting the group.

- ***usermod*** command is used to modify the membership of a user to a group. You can use the command *usermod -g groupname* to achieve the same.

  [student@desktop ~]$ sudo usermod -g student student

  You can add a user to the supplementary group using the *usermod -aG groupname username* command.

  [student@desktop ~]$ sudo usermod -aG wheel student

  Using the -a option ensures that modifications to the user are done in append mode. If you do not use it, you will be removed from all other groups and be only added to the new group.

User Password Management

In this section, we will learn about the shadow password file and how you can use it to manually lock accounts or set password-aging policies to an account. In the initial days of Linux development, the encrypted password for a user was stored in the file at /etc/passwd, which was world-readable. This was tested and found to be a secure path until attackers started using dictionary attacks on encrypted passwords. It was then that it was decided to move the location of encrypted password hash to a more secure location, which is at /etc/shadow file. The latest implementation allows you to set password-aging policies and expiration features using this new file.

The modern password hash has three pieces of information in it. Consider the following password hash:

1gCLa2/Z$6Pu0EKAzfCjxjv2hoLOB/

1. **1**: This part specifies the hashing algorithm used. The number 1 indicates that an MD5 hash has been implemented. The number **6** comes into the hash when a SHA-512 hash is used.

2. **gCLa2/Z**: This indicates the salt used to encrypt the hash. It is a randomly chosen salt at first. The combination of the unencrypted password and salt together form the encrypted hash. The advantage of having a salt is that two users who may be using the same password will not have identical hash entries in the /etc/shadow file.

3. **6Pu0EKAzfCjxjv2hoLOB/**: This is the encrypted hash.

In the event of a user trying to log in to the system, the system looks up for their entry in the /etc/shadow file. It then combines the unencrypted password entered by the user with the salt for the user and uses the hash algorithm specified to encrypt this combination. It is implied that the password typed by the user is correct of this hash matches with the hash in the /etc/shadow file. Otherwise, the user has just typed in the wrong password and their login attempt fails. This method is secure as it allows the system to determine if a user typed in the correct password without having to store the actual unencrypted password in the file system.

The format of the /etc/shadow file is as below. There are 9 fields for every user as follows.

name:	password:	lastchange:	minage:	maxage:	warning:	inactive:	expire:	blank

name: This must be a valid username on the system through, which a user logs in.

password: This is where the encrypted password of the user is stored. If the field starts with an exclamation mark, it means that password is locked.

lastchange: This is the timestamp of the last password change done for the account.

minage: This defines the minimum number of days before a password needs to be changed. If it is the number 0, it means there is no minimum age for the account.

maxage: This defines the maximum number of days before a password needs to be changed.

warning: This is a warning period that shows that the password is going to expire. If the number is 0, it means that no warning will be given before password expiry.

inactive: This is the number of days after password expiry the account will stay inactive. During this, the user can use the expired password and still log into the system to change his password. If the user fails to do so in the specified number of days for this field, the account will get locked and become inactive.

expire: This is the date when the account is set to expire.

blank: This is a blank field, which is reserved for future use.

Password Aging

Password aging is a technique that is employed by system administrators to safeguard bad passwords, which are set by users of an organization. The policy will basically set a number of days, which is 90 days by default after, which a user will be forced to change their password. The advantage of forcing a password change implies that even if someone has gained access to a user's password, they will have it with them only for a limited amount of time. The con to this approach is that users will keep writing their password in some place since they can't memorize it if they keep changing it.

In Red Hat Enterprise Linux 7, there are two ways through, which password aging can be enforced.

1. Using the chage command on the command line
2. Using the User Management application in the graphical interface

The **chage** command with the **-M** option lets a system admin specify the number of days for, which the password is valid. Let us look at an example.

[student@desktop ~]$ sudo chage -M 90 alice

In this command, the password validity for the user alice will be set to 90 days after, which the user will be forced to reset their password. If you want to disable password aging, you can specify the -M value as 9999, which is equivalent to 273 years.

You can set password aging policies by using the graphical user interface as well. There is an application called User Manager, which you can access from the Main Menu Button > System Settings > Users & Groups. Alternatively, you can type the command **system-config-users** in the terminal window. The User Manager window will pop up. Navigate to the Users tab, select the required user from the list, and click on the Properties button where you can set the password aging policy.

Access Restriction

You can set the expiry for an account using the **chage** command. The user will not be allowed to login to the system once that date is reached. You can use the **usermod** command with the **-L** option to lock a particular user account.

[student@desktop ~]$ sudo usermod -L alice

[student@desktop ~]$ su - alice

Password: alice

su: Authentication failure

The usermod command is useful to lock and expire an account at the same time in a case where the employee might have left the company.

[student@desktop ~]$ sudo usermod -L -e 1 alice

A user may not be able to authenticate into the system using a password once their account has been locked. It is one of the best practices to prevent authentication of an employee to the system who has already left the organization. You can use the **usermod -u** *username* command later to unlock the account, in the event that the employee has rejoined the organization. While doing this, if the account was in an expired state, you will need to ensure that you set a new expiry date for the account as well.

The nologin shell

There will be instances where you want to create a user who can authenticate using a password and get a login into the system but would not need a shell to interact with the system. For example, a mail server may require a user to have an email account so that the user can login and check their emails. But it is not necessary that the user needs a login to the system to check their emails.

This is where the nologin shell comes as a solution. What we do is we specify the shell for this user to point to **/sbin/nologin**. Once this is done, the user cannot login to the system using the direct login procedure.

[root@desktop ~]# usermod - s /sbin/nologin student

[root@desktop ~]# su - student

Last login: Tue Mar 5 20:40:34 GMT 2015 on pts/0

The account is currently not available.

By using the nologin shell for the user, you are denying the user interactive login into the system but not all access to the system. The user will still be able to use certain web applications for file transfer applications to upload or download files.

CHAPTER 5

Accessing Files in Linux and File System Permissions

In this chapter, we will learn about the working of the Linux file system permissions model and how the permissions and ownership of files can be changed using the command line tools available to us. By the end of the chapter, we will be well versed with how file permissions affect files in Linux and how permissions can be used to employ security to files and directories.

Linux File System Permissions

File Permissions is a feature in Linux through, which the access to a file by a user can be controlled. Although the Linux file system model is simple, it is still flexible in nature, which makes it easy for a new user to understand and apply it and handle file permissions in an easy manner.

There are three categories of users to, which permissions apply with respect to a file. The three categories of file users are as follows.

1. user
2. group
3. other

The hierarchy is such that user permissions will override group permissions, which will override other permissions.

The permissions that apply to a file or directory also belong to three categories.

1. read
2. write
3. execute

Let us see their effects on a file or a directory.

Permission	Effect on Files	Effect on Directories
r (read)	Read access to file content	Contents of a directory that is filenames will be listed.
w (write)	Write access to file content	Contents of the directory that is files can be created or deleted.
x (execute)	The file can be executed as a command	Contents of the directory can be accessed subject to the permission of the file itself.

A user is given read and execute access to a file by default so that they can read the content of the file and execute the file if it is an executable file. However, if a user has only read only access, they will only be able to read the contents of the file but no other information at all such as permissions of the file, timestamps, etc. If there is only an execute access for a user to the file, they will not be able to list the filename down in a directory, but if they already know the name of the file, they will be able to execute the file in a command.

If a user has write permissions to a directory, they have all rights to delete any file in that directory irrespective of the actual permissions on the file itself. There is, however, an exception to this where this can be overridden by special permission, known as the sticky bit, which we will discuss later in this chapter.

Let us now see how you can view the permissions, which are assigned to a file or a directory along with the ownership. You can use the **ls** command with the **-l** option to list down the files and directories along with their permissions and ownerships.

[student@desktop ~]$ ls -l test

-rw-rw-r--. 1 student student 0 Feb 5 15:45 test

Using the **ls -l directoryname** command, you can list down all the contents of the directory with additional information of permissions, ownerships, timestamps, etc. If you wish to see the listing of the parent directory itself and not descend down to the contents of the directory, you can use the **-d** option.

[student@desktop ~]$ ls -ld /home

drwxr-xr-x. 5 root root 4096 Feb 8 17:45 /home

If you have been using a Windows system, you will realize that the List Folder Contents permission from Windows is the equivalent of the Linux Read permission, and the Windows Modify permission is the equivalent of the Linux Write permission.

Windows has a feature called Full Control which is the equivalent of the power that the Root user has with respect to files and directories in Linux.

Managing File System Permissions using the Command Line

In this section, we will learn how we can use the command line in Linux to manage the permissions and ownerships for a file.

Changing the permissions of files and directories

The command we can use to change the permissions of files in Red Hat Enterprise Linux 7 from the command line is **chmod**, which is the short form for change mode since permissions are also referred to as the mode of a file or directory. The syntax of the command is followed by an instruction as to what needs to be changed and then the name of the file or directory on, which the operation needs to be executed. You can provide the instruction in two ways, that is, either numerically or symbolically.

Let us first go through the symbolic method and the syntax looks like this

chmod WhoWhatWhich files|directory

- Who is the user u, group g, other o and a for all
- What is + to add, - to remove, = to set exactly
- Which is r for read, w for write, and x for execute

You will use letter to specify the different groups that you wish to change the permissions for. u is for the user , g is for the group, o is for other, and a is for all.

When you are setting the permissions using the symbolic method, you do not need to specify a new set of permissions for the file. You can rather just make changes to the existing permissions. You can achieve this by using the three symbols +, - and =to add permissions to a set, remove permissions to a set or replace the entire set for a group of permissions respectively.

Lastly, the permissions are represented by using the letters where r is for read, w is for write, and x is for execute. Note that if you are using the chmod command with the symbolic method, and use a capital **X** as a permission flag, it will add the execute permission only if the file is a directory or already has an execute permission set for user u, group g, or other o.

Let us first go through the numeric method and the syntax looks like this

chmod ### files|directory

- Every position of the # represents an access level viz. User, group, and other

- # is the sum of read r=4, write w=2, execute x=1

In this method, we can set up permissions for files and directories using 3 digits(and sometimes 4 for special permissions) known as an octal number. A single digit can specify the number between 0-7, which shows the exact number of possibilities we can have with read, write and execute values.

Ig we understand the mapping between symbolic and numeric values, we will learn how yo do the conversion between the two as well. In the numeric representation, which is done by three digits, each digit represents permissions for a group. If we start from left to right, the first bit is for user, the second bit is for group and the third bit is for other. And for each of these groups, we can use a combination of the the read write and execute values, which are 4, 2 and 1 respectively.

Let us look at a symbolic representation of permissions, which is - **rwxr-x---**

In this representation, the user has the permissions of **rwx, which** is read write and execute. If we convert this to numeric form, it will be read r 4 + write w 2 + execute x 1, which is a total of 7.

Next for the group, we see that the permissions in symbolic form are **r-x, which** is to only read and execute. If we convert this to numeric form, it will be read r 4 + execute x 1, which is a total of 5.

The permission for others is ---, which means read write and execute are all 0. This means the other bit will be 0.

We can now say that the complete permission for all groups to this file in numeric format is represented as **750**.

We can also to a converse operation on this and do a conversion from numeric format to symbolic format.

Consider the permission **640**.

We know that the user bit is the left most bit, which is 6. The only combination of read, write and execute that will give us a 6 is that of read r 4 + write w 2. This means that the permission for the user in symbolic format is **rw-**.

Next the group bit is 4 and the only combination of read, write and execute that will give us a 4 is that of read r 4. This means that the permission for the group in symbolic format is **r--**.

Next the other bit is 0 and the only combination of read, write and execute that will give us a 0 is if values for read, write and execute are all 0. This means that the permission for the group in symbolic format is ---.

As a whole, the permission for this file in symbolic format will look like **-rw-r-----**.

Note: You can use the **-R** option with the **chmod** command if you want to set the same permissions recursively for all files under a directory tree. It is also noteworthy that while doing this, you can use the **X** flag symbolically to set the permissions of all directories so that they are accessible and that you can skip files while doing so.

Changing the user and group ownership of files and directories

By default, if a file is newly created, it is owned by the user who created the file. The default group ownership of that file is also associated by default to the primary group of the user who created it. Since Red Hat Enterprise Linux 7 has the concept of user private groups, the group will mostly be a group, which has only one member who is the user themselves. Access to files and directories can be granted by changing their owner and group.

You can use the **chown** command to change the ownership of a file or a directory. Let us see an example.

[root@desktop ~]# chown student newfile

In the example above, we are changing the user owner of the file newfile to student.

You can also use the option **-R** with the chown command, which will recursively change the ownership of a directory and all its files and subdirectories. The command can be used as shown below.

[root@desktop ~]# chown -R student parentdirectory

We can also use the chown command to change the group ownership of files and directories. The command is to be followed by the group name preceded by the colon :

Let us look at an example.

[root@desktop ~]# chown :admins newfile

This will change the group ownership of the file newfile to admins.

You can also use the chown command to change the user ownership and group ownership at the same time. The syntax for it is as follows.

[root@desktop ~]# chown student:admins newfile

This will change the user ownership to student and group ownership to admins for the file newfile.

The ownership of files and directories can only be changed by the root user. However, the group ownership of a file can be changed both by the root and the actual user who owns that file. Non-root users have access to provide ownership to groups that they are part of.

Note: An alternate command to the chown command is the **chgrp** command, which can be used to change the group ownership of a file or directory. The chgrp command works exactly the same way as the chown command and also works with the -R option to recursively change group ownership.

Managing File Access and Default Permissions

In this section, we are going to learn about special permissions. We will create a directory under, which files that will be created will have write access for users of the group that owns the directory by default. This will be achieved using the special permissions known as sticky bits.

Let us see how we can use the special permissions and apply them. There is a bit known as the **setuid** and **setgid** on the permissions, which allows an executable file to run as the user of that file or the group of that file and not as the user that ran the actual command.

One such example is the **passwd** file. Let us have a look at it.

[student@desktop ~]$ ls -l /usr/bin/passwd

-rw**s**r-xr-x. 1 root root 34598 Jul 15 2011 /usr/bin/passwd

The sticky bit for any file in the permissions sets a restriction on file deletions. Only the user who owns the file and the root user can delete the file. An example of this is /tmp.

[student@desktop ~]$ ls -ld /tmp

drwxrwxrw**t** 39 root root 4096 Jul 10 2011 /tmp

Lastly, the setgit bit is a bit that allows all files created within a directory to inherit the permissions of the directory rather than getting it set by the user who created the file. Group collaborative directories mostly use this feature to change file permissions from the default private group to shared groups.

Let us go through the effects of special permissions on files and directories.

Special Permission	Effect on Files	Effect on Directories
u+s suid	The file will execute as the user who owns the file and not the user who ran the command	No effect
g+s sgid	File executes as the group that owns the file	The group owner of the newly created file in the directory will match the group owner of the directory
o+t sticky	No effect	Users who have write access on the directory can only delete files owned by them. They cannot delete or force writes to files owned by other users

Let us see how we can set special permissions on files and directories.

- Symbolically, setuid is u+s, setgid is g+s and sticky is o+t
- Numerically, the special permissions use the fourth bit that precedes every user's first digit. setuid is 4, setgid is 2 and sticky is 1.

Let us now try and understand what default file permissions are. The permissions set for files by default are the ones that are set by the processes that created those files. For example, if you are using a text editor like Vim to create a file, the file will have read and write access for everyone but no execute access. Shell redirection follows the same rule. Additionally, compilers can create files that are binary executable in nature. Therefore, the files will have executable permissions. The mkdir command is used to create directories and these directories have all permissions for read, write and execute.

Research and experience has shown that the permissions on files and directories are not set when they are created because the **umask** of the shell process clears these permissions. If you use the umask command without any arguments, it will show the value of the current umask of the shell.

[student@desktop ~]$ umask

0002

There is a umask for every process on the system. The umask is basically an octal bitmask that clears the permissions of newly created files and directories that are created by a process. If the umask has a bit set, the corresponding permission is cleared in newly created files.

Let us take an example. The bitmask value shown above is 0002 where the bit for other users is 2. We know by this that the special, user and group permissions will not be cleared since those bits are all 0. Therefore permissions for other users will be cleared since the corresponding umask bit is 2. We assume that there are zeroes that lead if the umask is less than three digits.

The default umask values in the system for users of bash shell are defined at /etc/profile and /etc/bashrc file. The system defaults can be overridden by the users in their .bash_profile and .bashrc files.

CHAPTER 6

Linux Process Management

In this chapter, we will learn how to monitor and manage processes that run on Red Hat Enterprise Linux 7. By the end of this chapter, we will be able to list processes and interpret basic information about them on the system, use bash job control to control processes, use signals to terminate processes, and monitor system resources and system load caused by processes.

Processes

In this section, we will define the cycle of a typical process and understand the different states of a process. We will also learn to view and interpret processes.

What is a process?

An executable program in a state where it is running after being launched is called a process. A process has the following features.

- Allocated memory that points to an address space

- Properties with respect to security, which include ownership privileges and credentials

- Program code that contains one or more executable threads

- The state of the process

The process environment has the following features

- Variables that are both local and global in nature

- A current scheduling context

- System resources allocated to it, which include network ports and file descriptors

An existing process is known as a parent process, which splits and duplicates its address space to create a child process. For security and tracking, a unique process ID known as PID is assigned to every new process. The PID and the parent process's ID known as PPID together make the environment for the child process. A child process can be created by any process. All the processes in the system descend from the very first process of the system, which is known as **systemd** on Red Hat Enterprise Linux 7.

As the child process splits from a parent process through a fork, properties such as previous and current file descriptors, security identities, port privileges, resource privileges, program code, environment variables are all inherited by the child process. Once these properties have been inherited, the child process can then execute its own program code. When a child process runs, the parent process goes to sleep by setting a request to a wait flag until the child process completes. Once the child process completes, it leaves the system and releases all system resources and environment it has previously locked, and what remains of it is known as a zombie. Once the child process leaves, the parent process wakes up again and clean the remaining bit and starts to run its own program code again.

Process States

Consider an operating system, which is capable of multitasking. If it has hardware with a CPU that has multiple cores, every core can be dedicated to one process at a given point in time. During runtime, the requirements of CPU and other resources keep changing for a given process. This leads to processes being in a state, which changes as per the requirements of the current circumstance.

Let us go through the states of a process one by one by looking at the table given below.

Name	Flag	State name and description
Running	R	TASK_RUNNING: The process is waiting or executing on the CPU. The process could be executing routines for the user or the kernel. It could also be in a queued state where it is getting ready to run known as the Running state.
Sleeping	S	TASK_INTERRUPTIBLE: The process is waiting for a condition such as system resources access, hardware request, or a signal. When the condition is met by an event or signal, the process will get back to Running.
	D	TASK_UNINTERRUPTIBLE: The process is in the Sleeping state here as well, but unlike **S**, in this it will not respond to any signals. It is used only in specific conditions where an unpredictable device state can be caused due to process interruption.

	K	TASK_KILLABLE: It is much like the uninterruptible **D** state, but the task that is waiting can respond to a signal to be killed. Killable processes are displayed as the **D** state by utilities.
Stopped	T	TASK_STOPPED: The process is in a Stopped state because of another signal or process. Another signal can, however, send the process back into the Running state.
	T	TASK_TRACED: A process is in a state of being debugged and is therefore in a Stopped state. It shares the same **T** flag.
Zombie	Z	EXIT_ZOMBIE: A child process is complete, and it leaves the system and lets the parent process know about it. All resources held by the child process are released except for it process ID PID.
	X	EXIT_DEAD: The parent process has cleaned up the remains of the child process after it has exited, the child process has now been released completely. This state is rarely observed in utilities that list processes.

Listing processes

The current processes in the system can be listed using the **ps** command at shell prompt. The command provides detailed information about processes, which include:

- The UID user identification, which determines the privileges of the process

- The unique process ID PID
- The real time usage of the CPU
- The allocated memory by the process in various locations of the system
- The location of the process STDOUT standard output, known as the controlling terminal
- The current state of the process

The option **aux** can be used with the ps command, which will display detailed information of all the processes. It includes columns, which are useful to the user and also shows processes, which are without a controlling terminal. If you use the long listing option **lax**, you will get some more technical details, but it may display faster skipping the lookup of the username.

If you run the ps command without any options, it will display processes, which have the same effective user ID EUID as that of the current user and associated with the same terminal where the ps command was invoked.

- The ps listing also shows zombies, which are either exiting or defunct
- ps command only shows one display. You can alternatively use the top command, which will keep repeating the display output in realtime
- Process, which have round brackets are usually the ones run by kernel threads. They show up at the top of the listing
- The ps command can display a tree format so that you can understand the parent and child process relationships

- The default order in, which the processes are listed is not sorted. They are listed in a manner where the first process started, and the rest followed. You may feel that the output is chronological, but there is no guarantee unless you explicitly use options like -O or --sort

Controlling Jobs

In this section, we will learn about the terms such as foreground, background and the controlling terminal. We will also learn about using job control, which will allow us to manage multiple command line tasks.

Jobs and Sessions

Job control is a feature in shell through, which multiple commands can be managed by a single shell instance.

Every pipeline that you enter at the shell prompt is associated with a job. All processes in this pipeline are a part of the job and are members of the same process group. A minimal pipeline is when only a single command is entered on the shell prompt. In such a case, that command ends up being the only member of the job.

At a given time, inputs given to the command line from a keyboard can be read by only one job. That terminal is known as the controlling terminal and the processes that are a part of that job are known as foreground processes.

If there is any other job associated with that controlling terminal of, which it is a member, it is known as the background process of that controlling terminal. Inputs given from the keyboard to the terminal cannot be read by background processes, but they can still write to the terminal. A background job can be in a stopped state or a running state. If a background process tries to read from the terminal, the process gets automatically suspended.

Every terminal that is running is a session of its own and can have processes that are in the foreground and the background. A job is a part of one session only, the session that belongs to its controlling terminal.

If you use the **ps** command, the listing will show the name of the device of the controlling terminal of a process in a column named **TTY**. There are some processes started by the system, such as system daemons, which are not a part of the shell prompt. Therefore, these processes are not part of a job, or they do not have a controlling terminal and will never come to the foreground. Such processes, when listed using the ps command shows **?** mark in the TTY column.

Running Background Jobs

You can add an ampersand **&** to the end of a command line, which will run the command in the background. There will be a unique job number assigned to the job, and a process ID PID will be assigned to the child process, which is created in bash. The shell prompt will show up again after the command is executed as the shell will not wait for the child process to complete since it is running in the background.

[student@desktop ~]$ sleep 10000 &

[1] 5683

[student@desktop ~]$

Note: When you are putting a pipeline in the background with an ampersand **&**, the process ID PID that will show up in the output will be that of the last command in the pipeline. All other command that precede will be a part of that job.

[student@desktop ~]$ example_command | sort |mail -s "sort output" &

[1] 5456

Jobs are tracked in the bash shell, per session, in the output table that is shown by using the **jobs** command.

[student@desktop ~]$ jobs

[1]+ Running   sleep   10000 &

[student@desktop ~]$

You can use the **fg** command with a job ID(*%job number*) to bring a job from the background to the foreground.

[student@desktop ~]$ fg %1

sleep 10000

-

In the example seen above, we brought the sleep command, which was running in the background to the foreground on the controlling terminal. The shell will go back to sleep until this child process completes. This is why you will have to wait until the sleep command is over for the shell prompt to show up again.

You can send a process from the foreground to the background by pressing **Ctrl+z** on the keyboard, which will send a suspend request.

sleep 10000

^Z

[1]+   Stopped   sleep   10000

[student@desktop ~]$

The job will get suspended and will be placed in the background.

The information regarding jobs can be displayed using the **ps j** command. The display will show a PGID, which is the PID of the process group leader and refers to the first job in the pipeline of the job. The SID is the is the PID of the session leader, which with respect to a job refers to the interactive shell running on the controlling terminal.

[student@desktop ~]$ ps j

PPID	PID	PGID	SID	TTY	TPGID	STAT	UID	TIME
		COMMAND						
2434	2456	2456	2456	pts/0	5677	T	1000	0:00
	sleep 10000							

The status of the sleep command is T because it is in the suspended state.

You can start a suspended process again the in background and put it into a running state by using the **bg** command with the same job ID.

[student@desktop ~]$ bg %1

[1]+   sleep 10000 &

[student@desktop ~]$

If there are jobs that are suspended and you try to exit the shell, you will get a warning that will let you know that there are suspended jobs in the background. If you confirm to leave, the suspended jobs are killed immediately.

Killing Processes

In this section, we will learn how to use command to communicate with processes and kill them. We will understand what is a daemon process and what are its characteristics. We will also learn how to end processes and sessions owned by a user.

Using signals to control processes

A signal is an interrupt developed through software to be sent to a process. Events are sent to a program with the help of signals. These events that generate a signal can be external events, errors, or explicit requests such as commands sent using the keyboard.

Let us go through a few signals, which are useful for system admins in their routine day to day system management activities.

Signal number	Short name	Definition	Purpose
1	HUP	Hangup	This signal reports the termination of the controlling process in a terminal. Process reinitialization or configuration reload can be requested using this signal without any termination.
2	INT	Keyboard Interrupt	This signal lead to termination of a program. The signal can either be blocked or handled. The signal is sent by using the **Ctrl+c** on the keyboard known as **INTR**
3	QUIT	Keyboard quit	The signal is similar to **SIGINT** with the difference that a process dump is generated at termination. The signal is sent

				by using the **Ctrl+** on the keyboard known as **QUIT**
9	KILL	Kill, unblockable		This signal leads to an abrupt termination of the program. It cannot be blocked, handled, or ignored and is always fatal.
15 default	TERM	Terminate		This signal leads to termination of the program. Unlike **SIGKILL,** this signal can be clocked, ignored, or handled. This is requesting a program to terminate in a polite way, which results in proper clean-up.
18	CONT	Continue		This signal is sent to a process that is in a stopped state such that it resumes. The signal cannot be blocked, and process is resumed even if the signal is handled.
19	STOP	Stop, Unblockable		This signal leads to suspension of the process and cannot be handled or blocked.
20	TSTP	Keyboard stop		Unlike **SIGSTOP,** this signal can be blocked, handled, or ignored. The signal is sent by using the **Ctrl+z** on the keyboard known as **SUSP**

Note: The number of signal number can change based on the hardware being used for the Linux operating system, but the signal names and their purposes are standardized. Therefore, it is advisable that you use the signal names instead of the signal number on the command line. The signal numbers that we discussed above are only for systems that are associated with the Intel x86 architecture.

There is a default action associated with every signal, which corresponds to one of the following.

Term - The program is asked to exit or terminate at once.

Core - The program is asked to terminate but is asked to also save a memory image or a core dump before terminating.

Stop - the program is suspended or asked to stop and will have to wait to resume again.

Expected event signals can be tackled by programs by implementing routines for handlers so that they can replace, ignore, or extend the default action of a signal.

Commands used to send signals through explicit requests

Processes that are running in the foreground can be signaled using the keyboard by users, wherein control signals are sent to the process using keys like Ctrl+z for suspend, Ctrl+c for kill, and Ctrl+\ for getting a core dump. If you want to send signals to processes that are running in the background or are running in a different session altogether, you will need to use a command to send signals.

You can either use signal names(-HUP or -SIGHUP) to signal numbers(-1) to specify a signal. Processes, which are owned by a user can be killed by the users themselves, but processes owned by others will need root user privileges to be killed.

- The **kill** command can be sent to a process using the process ID PID. However, irrespective of the name, the kill command can be used to send other signals to a process as well and not just for sending a signal to terminate the process.

[student@desktop ~]$ kill PID
[student@desktop ~]$ kill -signal PID

- The **killall** command can be used to send a signal to multiple processes, which may match a given criteria such as processes owned by a particular user, command name, all system processes.

[student@desktop ~]$ killall command_pattern
[student@desktop ~]$ killall -signal command_pattern
[student@desktop ~]$ killall -signal -u username command_pattern

- Just like the **killall** command, there is another command called **pkill, which** can be used to signal multiple processes at the same time. The selection criteria used by pkill is advanced in comparison to killall and contains the following combinations.

Command - Pattern that is matched using the command name
UID - Processes that belong to a particular user matched using UID
GID - Processes that belong to a particular group matched using GID
Parent - Child processes that belong to a particular parent process
Terminal - Processes that are running on a particular controlling terminal

[student@desktop ~]$ pkill command_pattern
[student@desktop ~]$ pkill -signal command_pattern
[root@desktop ~]# pkill -G GID command_pattern
[root@desktop ~]# pkill -P PPID command_pattern
[root@desktop ~]# pkill -t terminal_name -U UID command_pattern

Administratively logging out users

The **w** command lists down all the users that are logged into the system and the processes that are being run by these users. You can determine the location of the users by analyzing the **FROM** and the **TTY** columns.

Every user is associated with a controlling terminal, which is indicated by **pts/N** while working on a graphical interface or **ttyN** while working on a system console where **N** is the number of the controlling terminal. Users who have connected remotely to the system will be displayed in the **FROM** column when you use the **-f** option.

[student@desktop ~]$ w -f

12:44:34 up 25 min, 1 users, load average: 0.06, 0.45, 0.55

USER	TTY	FROM	LOGIN@	IDLE	JCPU	PCPU	WHAT
student	pts/0	:0	12:32	2.02s	0.07s	0.07s	w -f

The session login time will let you know as to how long a user has been on the system. The CPU resources that are utilized by current jobs, including the child processes and background jobs are shown in the JCPU column. CPU utilization for foreground processes are shown in the PCPU column.

If a user is violating security of the system, or over-allocating resources, they can be forced out of the system. Therefore, if the system admin is requesting a user to close processes that are not required, close command shells that are unused, exit login sessions, they are supposed to follow the system admin.

In situations where a user is out of contact and has a ongoing sessions, which are putting a load on the system by consuming resources, a system admin may need to administratively end their session.

Note: The signal to be used in this case is **SIGTERM** but most system admins use **SIGKILL, which** can be fatal. The SIGKILL signal cannot be handled or ignored, it is fatal. Processes are forced to terminate without completing clean-up routines. Therefore, we recommend that you send the SIGTERM signal first before trying the SIGKILL signal when the process is not responding.

Signal can be sent individually or collectively to terminal or processes. You can use the **pkill** command to terminate all processes for a particular user. If you want to kill all the processes of a user and all their login shells, you will need to use the **SIGKILL** signal. This is because the session leader process, which is the initial process in a session, can handle session termination requests and other signals coming from the keyboard.

[root@desktop ~]# pgrep -l -u alice

6787 bash

6789 sleep

6999 sleep

7000 sleep

[root@desktop ~]# pkill -SIGKILL -u alice

[root@desktop ~]# pgrep -l -u alice

[root@desktop ~]#

If you need certain processes by a user and only want to kill a few of their other processes, it is not necessary to kill all their processes.

Use the **w** command and figure out the controlling terminal for the session and then use the terminal ID to kill processes from a terminal, which is not required. The session leader, which is the bash login shell will survive the termination command unless you use the SIGKILL command, but this will terminate all other session processes.

[root@desktop ~]# pgrep -l -u alice

6787 bash

6789 sleep

6999 sleep

7000 sleep

[root@desktop ~]# w -h -u alice

alice   tty3   18:54   5:07   0.45s   0.34s   -bash

[root@desktop ~]# pkill -t tty3

[root@desktop ~]# pgrep -l -u alice

6787 bash

[root@desktop ~]# pkill SIGKILL -t tty3

[root@desktop ~]# pgrep -l -u alice

The criteria of terminating processes selectively can also be applied by using arguments of relationships between parent and child processes. The **pstree** command can be used in this case. The pstree command shows a process tree for a user or for the system. You can kill all its child processes by passing the parent process's parent ID PID. The bash login shell of the parent process still remains since only the child processes are terminated.

[root@desktop ~]# pstree -u alice

bash(8341)───sleep(8454)

             ───sleep(8457)

             ───sleep(8459)

[root@desktop ~]# pkill -P 8341

[root@desktop ~]# pstree -l -u alice

bash(8341)

[root@desktop ~]# pkill -SIGKILL -P 8341

[root@desktop ~]# pstree -l -u alice

bash(8341)

[root@desktop ~]#

Process Monitoring

In this section, we will learn how to monitor processes in real time and how to interpret load averages on the CPU of the system.

Load Average

The Linux kernel is capable of calculating a **load average** metric, which is the **exponential moving average** of the **load number**, a cumulative count of the CPU that is kept in accordance with the system resources that are active in that given instance.

- Threads that are currently running or threads that are waiting for input or output are counted as the active requests in the CPU queue. Meanwhile, the kernel keeps track of the activity of process resources and the changes in the state of the process.

- The calculation routine run by default in the system at an interval of every five seconds is known as load number. The load number will accumulate and average out all the active requests into one single number for every CPU.

- The mathematical formula used to smoothen the highs and lows of trending data, the increase in significance of current activity, and decrease in the quality of aging data is known as the exponential moving average.

- The result of the routine load number calculation is known as load average. It refers to the display of 3 figures, which show the load averages for 1, 5 and 15 minutes.

Let us try and understand how the load average calculation works in Linux systems.

The load average is a perception of load received by the system over a period of time. Along with CPU, the load average calculation also takes into consideration the disk and the network input and output.

- Linux systems do not just count processes. The threads of a process are also counted individually and account as different tasks. The requests to CPU queues for running threads(nr_running) and threads that are waiting for I/O resources(nr_iowait) correspond to the process states of R Running and D Uninterruptible Sleeping. Tasks that may be sleeping are waiting for responses from disk and networks are included in tasks waiting for Input/Output I/O.

- All the CPUs of the system are taken into consideration and there the load number is known as the global counter for calculation. We cannot have counts that are accurate per CPU as tasks, which were initially sleeping, may be assigned to a different CPU when they resume. Therefore, we go for a count that has cumulative accuracy. The load average that is displayed represents all the CPUs.

- Linux will count each physical core of the CPU and microprocessor hyperthread as an execution unit, and therefore as an individual CPU. The request queues for each CPU is independent. You can check the /proc/cpuinfo file, which has all the information about the CPUs.

[root@desktop ~]# grep "model name" /proc/cpuinfo

model name: Intel(R) Core(TM) i5 CPU   M 2600 @ 2.60GHz

model name: Intel(R) Core(TM) i7 CPU   M 2600 @ 3.60GHz

model name: Intel(R) Core(TM) i7 CPU   M 2600 @ 3.60GHz

model name: Intel(R) Core(TM) i7 CPU   M 2600 @ 3.60GHz

[root@desktop ~]# grep "model name" /proc/cpuinfo |wc -l

4

- Previously known UNIX systems used to consider only CPU load or the length of the run queue to calculate the system load. But soon it was realized that a system would have CPUs that may be idle, but the other resources like disk and network could be busy and it was factored into the load average shown in modern Linux systems. If the load average is high despite minimal CPU activity, you may want to have a look at the disk and the network.

Let us now learn how we can interpret the values shown for load averages. This is an important part of being a system admin. As we have already seen, you will see three values, which are the load values over a time period of 1, 5, and 15 minutes. Having a quick look at these three values is enough to understand whether the load on the system is increasing or decreasing. We can then calculate the approximate value for per CPU load, which will let us know if the system is experiencing severe wait time.

- You can use the command line utilities of **top, uptime, w** and **gnome-system-monitor** to display values of average load.

- [root@desktop ~]# uptime
  15:30:45   up   14 min,   2 users,   load average: 2.56, 4.56, 5.76

- You can now divide the load average values that you see by the number of logical CPUs that are present in the system. If the result shows a value below 1, it implies that resources utilization and wait times are minimal. If the value is above 1, it indicates that resources are saturated and that there is waiting time.

- If the CPU queue is idle, then load number will be 0. Threads that are waiting or ready will add a count of 1 to the queue. If the total count on the queue is 1, resources of CPU, disk and network are busy, but there is no waiting time for other requests. With every additional request, the count increases by 1, but since many requests can be executed simultaneously, the resource utilization goes up but there is no wait time for other requests.

- The load average in increases by processes that may be in the sleeping state since they are waiting for input or output, but the disk and the network are busy. Although this does not mean that the CPU is being utilized, it still means that there are processes and users waiting for system resources.

- The load average will stay below 1 until all the resources begin to get saturated as tasks are seldom found to be waiting in the queue. It is only when requests start getting queued and are counted by the calculation routine that the load average starts spiking up. Every additional request coming in will start experiencing wait time when the resource utilization touches 100 percent.

Process monitoring in Real time

Much like the **ps** command, the **top** command gives a dynamic view of the processes in the system, which shows a header summary and list of threads and processes. The difference is that the output in the ps command is static in nature and just gives a one time output. The output of the top command is dynamic and keeps refreshing the values in real time. The interval at, which the values refresh can be customized. You can also configure other things such as sorting, column reordering, highlighting, etc. and these user configurations can be saved and are persistent.

The default output columns are as follows.

- The process ID **PID**

- The process owner that is the user name **USER**

- All the memory that is used by a process **VIRT**, which includes memory used by shared libraries, resident set, and memory pages that may be mapped or swapped.

- The physical memory used by a process known as resident memory **RES, which** includes memory used by shared objects.

- The state of the process **S** displays as
  D: Uninterruptible Sleeping
  R: Running or Runnable

S: Sleeping
T: Traced or Stopped
Z: Zombie

- The total processing time since the process began is known as CPU time **TIME**. It can be toggled so as to show the cumulative time of all the previous child processes.

- The command name process **COMMAND**

Let us now go through some keystrokes that are helpful for system admins while using the top display.

Key	Purpose
? or h	Display the help section
l, t, m	Header lines of memory, load and threads are toggled
1	Toggle to show individual CPU or all CPUs
s	Change the refresh rate of the screen in seconds
b	The default for running process is a bold highlight. This toggles reverse highlighting
B	Bold can be enabled in the header, display, and for running processes

H	Used to toggle threads to show individual threads or a summary of the processes
u, U	Used to filter for a username
M	Processes are sorted by memory usage in descending order
P	Processes are sorted by processor usage in descending order
k	Kills a process. When prompted, enter PID and signal
r	Renice a process. When prompted, enter PID and nice_value
w	Save or write the current display configuration when you launch top again
q	Quit

CHAPTER 7

Services and Daemons in Linux

In this chapter, we will learn now to control and monitor network related services and system daemons using the systemd utility. By the end of this chapter, you will be able to list system daemons and network services, which are started by the systemd service and socket units. You will also be able to control networking services and system daemons using the systemctl command line utility.

Identifying System Processes Started Automatically

In this section, we will learn about system processes such as system daemons and network services that are automatically invoked by the Linux system when it initiates the **systemd** service and socket units.

What is systemd?

When your Linux system boots up, all the processes that are invoked at startup are managed by **systemd**, which is the System and Service Manager. The program includes methods that call and activate system resources, server daemons, and other relevant processes, both when the system is booting up and then later running.

Processes that are waiting or running in the background and performing different tasks are known as **daemons**. Generally, daemons are invoked automatically during the boot process. and they shut down only when the system shuts down, or if they are stopped exclusively. The naming convention for any daemon maintains that the name of the daemon ends with the letter **d**.

A socket is something that is used by a daemon to listen to connections. A socket is the primary channel for communication with both local and remote clients. A daemon can create a socket and can be separated from the socket as well such that they get created by other processes like systemd. When a connection is established with the client, the daemon takes control over the socket.

A service implies one or more daemons. However, the state of the system may be changed as a one time process by starting or stopping a process. This does not involve keeping a daemon process in the running state afterward. This is known as **oneshot**.

Let us go through some history about how systemd was created. For many years now, the process ID 1 in Linux system was dedicated to a process known as **init**. This is the process, which was invoked first during boot up and was responsible for starting all other processes and services on the system. The term "init system" got its origin from this process. The daemons that would be needed frequently would be initiated on the system at boot up by using the LSB init scripts. These scripts are shell scripts and you can expect variations based on the Linux system that you are on. If there were daemons, which were seldom used, they would be started by other services such as initd or xinetd, which listen to connections from clients. These previous systems had a lot of limitations and were later addressed by introducing systemd.

In Red Hat Enterprise Linux 7, the process ID 1 is assigned to systemd, which is the modern initd process. Let us go through the features of systemd one by one.

- The boot speed of the system was increased because of parallel processes.

- Daemons could be started on demand without needing other services to start them.

- Linux control groups, which made way for tracking related processes together.

- Service dependency management was automated, which helped reduce timeouts by preventing a network service from starting when it was not available.

systemd and systemctl

Different types of systemd objects known as units can be managed using the systemctl command. You can use the **systemctl -t help** command to list down all the unit types. Let us go through a few common unit types.

- Service units, which represent services of the system have a .service extension. This unit will be used to start daemons like a web server, which are frequently accessed.

- The inter process communication sockets IPC are represented y socket units, which have the .service extension. When a connection is made by the client, the control of the socket is transferred to the daemon. At booth time, the start of a service can be delayed using socket units or to start services, which are not used very frequently.

- Path units, which have the extension .path are used to delay the initiation of a service until a desired change occurs in the file system. This is used for services, which use the spool directory such as the printer service.

Service states

The command **systemctl service name.type** can be used to view the status of a service. If the tpe of the unit is not provided, systemctl will show the status of a service unit.

The output of the command has certain keywords that are interesting to a system admin, which will indicate the state of a service. Let us go through these keywords one by one.

Keyword	Description
loaded	The unit configuration file has been processed
active (running)	The service is running and has one or more processes continuing
active (exited)	A one time configuration has been executed successfully
active (waiting)	Service is in running state but is waiting for an event
inactive	Not running
enabled	The service will start at boot time
disabled	The service will not start at boot time
static	Can not be enabled but can be started automatically by another enable unit

Note: The **systemctl status NAME** command replaces the command **service NAME status, which** was used in the previous version of Red Hat Enterprise Linux.

Let us go through an example where we will list files using the systemctl command

1. Verify the system startup by querying the state of all units
   [root@desktop ~]# systemctl

2. Query the state of service units only
   [root@desktop ~]# systemctl --type=service

3. Check units, which are in the maintenance or failed state. Use the -l option to show full output

   [root@desktop ~]# systemctl status rngd.service –l

4. The status argument can be passed to see if a service is active or if it will be made active during the boot process. There are alternative commands to show the active or enabled states as well

   [root@desktop ~]# systemctl is-active sshd
   [root@desktop ~]# systemctl is-enabled sshd

5. List the active state of all units that are currently loaded. You can also filter the type of unit. Additionally, you can use the --all option to show unites that are inactive as well

   [root@desktop ~]# systemctl list-units --type=service
   [root@desktop ~]# systemctl list-units --type=service --all

6. View the setting for all units with respect to enabled or disabled. As an option, filter the type of unit

   [root@desktop ~]# systemctl list-unit-files --type=service

7. Show only failed units

   [root@desktop ~]# systemctl --failed --type=service

Controlling System Services

In this section, we will learn how to control network services and system daemons using the systemctl command line utility.

Starting and Stopping system daemons

When you make changes to a configuration file of a service, it is necessary that you restart the service for those changes to be reflected in the system. A service that you do not wish to use anymore can be stopped before you uninstall the software that is related to the service. As a system admin, you may sometimes want to start a service manually only when it is needed. We will go through an example, which will show you how to start, stop, and restart a service.

1. Firstly, let us see the status of a service
   [root@desktop ~]# systemctl service sshd.service

2. Let us check if the service is in the running state
   [root@desktop ~]# ps -up PID

3. Let us now stop the service and check its status
   [root@desktop ~]# systemctl stop sshd.service
   [root@desktop ~]# systemctl status sshd.service

4. Let us now start the service again and check its status. Also notice that the process ID PID would have changed for the service
   root@desktop ~]# systemctl start sshd.service
   root@desktop ~]# systemctl status sshd.service

5. Stop the service and then start it again using just one command
   root@desktop ~]# systemctl restart sshd.service
   root@desktop ~]# systemctl status sshd.service

6. Without making the service stop and start again completely, make the service read the new configuration in the configuration file. This will not change the process ID PID
   root@desktop   ~]#   systemctl   reload   sshd.service
   root@desktop ~]# systemctl status sshd.service

Some service may start as dependencies of other services. If there is a socket unit that is enabled, but a service unit is not available with the same name, the service will start automatically when there is a request made at the network socket. When a condition for file system is met, services may also get triggered by path units. For example, if you are placing a file in the print spool directory, it will automatically start the cups service if it was not already running.

root@desktop ~]# systemctl stop cups.service

Warning: Stopping cups, but it can be activated by:

cups.path

cups.socket

You will need to stop all three units in order to stop printing on the system completely. You can disable the service, which will, in turn, disable its dependencies. The command **systemctl list-dependencies UNIT** can be used to print out a tree, which will show all the other units that need to be started in order for the specified unit to work. Depending upon the need, the dependency may need to already be in a running state or start after the specified uni has started. Conversely, if you use the **--reverse** option with a specified unit, you will come to know, which other units need the specified unit as a dependency for them to run.

There will be times when there are conflicting services that are installed on the system. For example, networks can be managed via different methods such as NetworkManager and network. Also, firewalls can be managed using a couple of services such as firewalld and iptales. A network service can be masked to prevent it from starting accidentally by a system admin. When you mask a service, a link is created for the service in its configuration directory such that nothing happens even if you launch it.

root@desktop ~]# systemctl mask network

Ln -s '/dev/null' '/etc/systemd/system/network.service'

root@desktop ~]# systemctl unmask network

Rm '/etc/systemd/system/network.service'

Note: A services that has been disabled will not launch automatically at boot process. It needs to be started manually. Also, a masked service cannot be started manually or automatically.

Enabling System Daemons to Start or Stop at Boot

When you start a service on a system that is already up and running does not guarantee that the service will start automatically again when you restart the system. Conversely, if you manually stop a service when the system was up would not mean that will not start again automatically if the system is restarted. When you create appropriate links in the systemd configuration directories, services are automatically started during the system's boot process. The systemctl command is used to create and delete these links.

Let us go through some examples, which will give us an idea about how to make system daemons start or stop during the boot process.

1. Let us first view the status of a service
   [root@desktop ~]# systemctl service sshd.service

2. Let us now disable the service and check its status. The service does not stop if you disable it

root@desktop ~]# systemctl disable sshd.service
root@desktop ~]# systemctl status sshd.service

3. Let us enable the service again and check its status
root@desktop ~]# systemctl enable sshd.service
root@desktop ~]# systemctl is-enabled sshd.service

Let us summarize all the **systemctl** commands that we have learned. Systemctl command helps to start or stop a service or enable or disable a service during boot time.

Task	Command
Get a unit's state's detailed information	systemctl status UNIT
Stop a service on a running system	systemctl stop UNIT
Start a service on a running system	systemctl start UNIT
Restart a service on a running system	systemctl restart UNIT
Reload the configuration file of a running service	systemctl reload UNIT
Disable a service from starting at boot or manually	systemctl mask UNIT
Make a masked service available	systemctl unmask UNIT
Enable a service to start at boot	systemctl enable UNIT
Disable a service from starting at boot	systemctl disable UNIT
List dependencies of a particular unit	systemctl list-dependencies UNIT

CHAPTER 8

OpenSSH Service

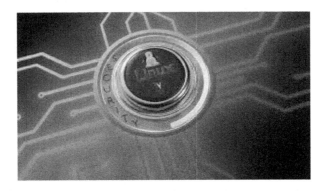

In this chapter, we will learn how to configure and secure the openSSH service. The openSSH service is used to access Linux systems using the command line. By the end of this chapter, we will learn how to log into a remote system using SSH and how to run a command on the shell prompt of the remote system. We will also learn how to configure the SSH service to implement password free login between two systems by using a private key file for authentication. We will learn how to make SSH secure by configuring it to disable root logins and to disable password based authentication as well.

Using SSH to Access the Remote Command Line

In this section, we will learn how we can log in to a remote system using ssh and run commands on the shell prompt of the remote system.

What is OpenSSH secure shell (SSH)?

The term OpenSSh refers to the software implementation in Linux systems known as Secure Shell. The terms OpenSSH, ssh, Secure Shell, which are synonymous with each other is an implementation that lets you run shell on a remote system in a very secure manner. If you have a user configured for you on a remote Linux system, which also has SSH services, you can remotely login to the system using ssh. You can also run a single command on a remote Linux system using the ssh command.

Let us go through some example of the secure shell. They will give you an idea of the syntax used for remote logins and how to run commands on the remote shell.

- Login using ssh on a remote shell with the current user and then use the exit command to return to your original shell
  [student@desktop ~]$ ssh remotesystem
  stident@remotesystem's password:
  [student@remotesystem ~]$ exit
  Connection to remotesystem closed.
  [student@desktop ~]$

- Connect to a remote shell as a different user (remoteuser) on a remote system
  [student@desktop ~]$ ssh remoteuser@remotesystem
  remoteuser@remotesystem's password:
  [remoteuser@remotesystem ~]$

- Execute a single command on the remote system as a remote user
  [student@desktop ~]$ ssh remoteuser@remotesystem hostname
  remoteuser@remotesystem's password
  remotesystem.com
  [student@desktop ~]$

The **w** command that we learned about previously displays all the users that are currently logged into the system. The FROM column of the output of this command will let you know if the user who is logged in is from the local system or from a remote system.

SSH host keys

The communication between two systems via ssh is secured through public key encryption. A copy of the public key is sent by the server to the client before the ssh client connects to the server. This method is used to complete the authentication of the server to the client and also to set up a connection using secure encryption.

When you try to ssh into a remote system for the first time, the ssh command stores the public key of the server in your ~/.ssh/known_hosts file. Every time after this, when you try to login to the remote system, the server sends a public key and compares it to the public key that is stored in you ~/.ssh/known_hosts file. If the keys match, a secure connection is established. If the keys do not match, it is assumed that the connection attempt was altered by some hijacking the connection and connection is closed immediately.

If the public key of the server is changed for reasons such as loss of data on the hard drive or if the hard drive was replaced for a genuine reason, you will need to remove the old entry of the server' public key from ~/.ssh/known_hosts file and replace it with the new public key.

- Host IDs are stored on your local system at ~/.ssh/known_hosts
  You can **cat** this file to see all the public keys of remote hosts stored on your local system.

- The keys of the host are stored on the SSH server at /etc/ssh/ssh_host_key*

SSH Based Authentication

In this section, we will learn how to setup a secure login via ssh without using password based authentication and by enabling key based logins using the private key authentication file.

SSH key based authentication

There is a way to authenticate ssh logins without using passwords through a method known as public key authentication. A private-public key pair scheme can be used by users to authenticate their ssh logins. There are two keys generated. One is a private key and a public key. The private key file must be kept secret and in a secure location as it is like a password credential. The public key is copied to the system that a user may want to login to and is used to verify and match with the private key. There is no need for the public key to be a secret. An SSh server, which has your public key stored on it can issue a challenge, which will only be met by a system that has your private key on it. Therefore, when you log in from your system to a server, your private key will be present on your system, which will match the public key on the server resulting into a secure authentication. This is a method that is secure and does not require you to type your password to login every time.

You can use the **ssh-keygen** command on your local system to generate your private and public key pair. The private key is then generated and kept at ~/.ssh/id_rsa and the public gey is generated and kept at ~/.ssh/id_rsa.pub.

Note: When you are generating your keys, you are given an option to set a passphrase as well. In the event that someone steals your private key, they will not be able to use your private key without a passphrase since only you would know the passphrase. This additional security measure will give you enough time to set a new key pair before the attacker cracks your private key, knowing that your existing private key is stolen.

Once you have generated the SSH keys, they will be stored in the user's home directory under /.ssh. You then need to copy your public key to the destination system with, which you want to establish key based authentication. You can do this by using the **ssh-copy-id** command.

[student@system1 ~]$ ssh-copy id student@system2

When you use the command **ssh-copy-id** to copy your public key from your system to another system, it automatically copies your public key from ~/.ssh/id_rsa.pub

Customizing the SSH Configuration

In this section, we will learn how to customize the sshd configuration such that we can restrict password based logins or direct logins.

It is not really necessary to configure the openSSH service but there are options available to customize it. All the parameters of the sshd service can be configured in the file that is located at /etc/ssh/sshd_config.

Prohibiting root user logins from SSH

With respect to security, it is advisable that we restrict the root user to login directly using the ssh service.

- The user name root is available on every Linux system. If you allow root logins, an attacker only needs to know the root user's password to be able to login as root via ssh. Therefore, it is good practice to not allow root logins via ssh at all.

- The root user is a super user with unlimited privileges, and therefore, it makes sense to not allow the root user to login using ssh.

The ssh configuration file has a line, which we can comment out to restrict root user logins. You need to edit the file /etc/ssh/sshd_config and comment out the following line:
#PermitRootLogin yes

When to comment out the line for permitting root login, the root user will not be able to login using the ssh service once the sshd service has been restarted.

PermitRootLogin no

For the changes in the configuration file to come into effect, you will need to restart the sshd service

root@desktop ~]# systemctl restart sshd

Another option available it to allow only key based login where you can edit the following line into the file.
PermitRootLogin without-password

Prohibiting password authentication during ssh

There are many advantages of allowing only key based logins to a remote system.

- The length of an SSH key is longer than a password and therefore, it is more secure.
- Once you have completed the initial setup, there is hardly any time taken for the future logins.

You need to edit the file /etc/ssh/sshd_config where there is a line that allows password authentication by default.

PasswordAuthentication yes

To stop password authentication, you need to edit this line to no and then restart the sshd service.

PasswordAuthentication no

Always make sure that after you have modified the sshd service configuration file at /etc/ssh/sshd_config you will need to restart the sshd service.

root@desktop ~]# systemctl restart sshd

CHAPTER 9

Log Analysis

In this chapter, we will learn how to locate logs in the Linux system and interpret them for system administration and troubleshooting purposes. We will describe the basic architecture of syslog in Linux systems and learn to maintain synchronization and accuracy for the time zone configuration such that timestamps in the system logs are correct.

Architecture of System Logs

In this section, we will learn about the architecture of system logs in Red Hat Enterprise Linux 7 system.

System logging

Events that take place as a result of processes running in the system and the kernel of the operating system need to be logged. The logs will help in system audits and to troubleshoot issues that are faced in the system. As a convention, all the logs in Linux based systems are stored at **/var/log** directory path.

Red Hat Enterprise Linux 7 has a system built for standard logging by default. This logging system is used by many programs. There are two services **systemd-journald** and **rsyslog, which** handle logging in Red Hat Enterprise Linux 7.

The **systemd-journald** collects and stores logs for a series of process, which are listed below.

- Kernel
- Early stages of the boot process
- Syslog
- Standard output and errors of various daemons when they are in the running state

All these activities are logged in a structural pattern. Therefore, all these events get logged in a centrally managed database. All messages relevant to syslog are also forwarded by **systemd-journald** to **rsyslog** to be processed further.

The messages are then sorted by rsyslog based on facility or type and priority and then writes them to persistent files in **/var/log** directory.

Let us go through all the types of logs, which are stored in /var/log based on the system and services.

Log file	Purpose
/var/log/messages	Most of the syslog messages are stored in this file with the exception of messages related to email processing and authentication, cron jobs and debugging related errors
/var/log/secure	Errors related to authentication and security are stored in this file
/var/log/maillog	Mail server related logs are stored in this file
/var/log/cron	Periodically executed tasks known are known as cron. Related logs are stored in this file

/var/log/boot.log	Messages that are associated with boot up are stored here

Syslog File Review

In this section, we will learn how to review system logs, which can help a system admin to troubleshoot system related issues.

Syslog files

The syslog protocol is used by many programs in the system to log their events. The log message is categorized by two things.

- Facility, which is the type of message
- Priority, which is the severity of the message

Let us go through an overview of the priorities one by one.

Code	Priority	Severity
0	emerg	The state of the system is unusable
1	alert	Immediate action needs to be taken
2	crit	The condition is critical
3	err	The condition is non-critical with errors
4	warning	There is a warning condition
5	notice	The event is normal but significant
6	info	There is an informational event
7	debug	The message is debugging-level

The method to handle these log messages is determined by the priority and the type of the message by rsyslog. This is already configured in the file at /etc/rsyslog.conf and by other conf files in /etc/rsyslog.d. As a system admin, you can overwrite this default configuration and customize the way rsyslog file to be able to handle these log messages as per your requirement. A message that has been handled by the rsyslog service can show up in many different log files. You can prevent this by changing the severity field to none so that messages directed to this service will not append to the specified log file.

Log file rotation

There is **logrotate** utility in place in Red Hat Enterprise Linux 7 and other linux variants so that log files do not keep piling up the /var/log file system and exhaust the disk space. The log file gets appended with the date of rotation when it is rotated. For example, and old file named /var/log/message will change to /var/log/messages-20161023 if the file was rotated on October 23, 2016. A new log file is created after the old log file is rotated and it is notified to the relevant service. The old log file is usually discarded after a few days, which is four weeks by default. This is done to free up disk space. There is a cron job in place to rotate the log files. Log files get rotated on a weekly basis, but this may vary based on the size of the log file and could be done faster or slower.

Syslog entry analysis

The system logs, which are logged by the rsyslog program have the oldest log message at the top of the file and the latest message at the end of the file. There is a standard format that is used to maintain log entries that are logged by rsyslog. Let us go through the format of the /var/log/secure log file.

Feb 12 11:30:45   localhost   sshd[1432]   Failed password for user from 172.25.0.11 port 59344 ssh2

- The first column shows the timestamp for the log entry

- The second column shows the host from, which the log message was generated

- The third column shows the program or process, which logged the event

- The final column shows the message that was actually sent

Using the tail command to monitor log files

It is a common practice for system admins to reproduce the issue so that error logs for the issue get generated in real time. The **tail -f /path/to/file** command can be used to monitor logs that are generated in real time. The last 10 lines of the log file are displayed with this command while it still continues to print new error logs that are generated in real time. For example, if you wanted to look for real time logs of failed login attempts, you can use the following tail command, which will help you see real time logs.

[root@desktop ~]# tail -f /var/log/secure

...

Feb 12 11:30:45 localhost sshd[1432] Failed password for user from 172.25.0.11 port 59344 ssh2

Using logger to send a syslog message

You can send messages to the rsyslog service by using the **logger** command. The command useful when you have made some changes to the configuration file of rsyslog and you want to test it. You can execute the following command, which will send a message that gets logged at /var/log/boot.log

[root@desktop ~]# logger -p local7.notice "Log entry created"

Reviewing Journal Entries for Systemd

In this section, we will learn to review the status of the system and troubleshoot problems by analyzing the logs in the systemd journal.

Using journalctl to find events:

The systemd journal uses a structured binary file to log data. Extra information about logged events is included in this data. For syslog events, this contains the severity and priority of the original message.

When you run **journalctl** as the root user, the complete system journal is shown, starting from the oldest log entry in the file.

Messages of priority notice or warning are highlighted in bold by the journalctl command. The higher priority messages are highlighted in red color.

You can use the journalctl command successfully to troubleshoot and audit is to limit the output of the command to only show relevant output.

Let us go through the various methods available to limit output of the journalctl command to show only desired output.

You can display the last 5 entries of the journal by using the following command.

[root@server ~]# journalctl -n 5

You can use the priority criteria to filter out journalctl output to help while troubleshooting issues. You can use the **-p** option with the journalctl command to specify a name or a number of the priority levels, which shows the entries that are of high level. journalctl know the priority levels such as info, debug, notice, err, warning, crit, emerg, and alert.

You can use the following command to achieve the above mentioned output.

[root@server ~]# journalctl -p err

There is command for journalctl similar to tail -f, which is **journalctl -f**. This will again list the last 10 lines of journal entry and then keep printing log entries in real time.

[root@server ~]# journalctl -f

You can also use some other filters to filter out journalctl entries as per your requirement. You can pass the following options of **--since** and **--until** to filters out journal entries as per timestamps. You need to then pass the arguments such as **today, yesterday** or an actual timestamp in the format **YYYY-MM-DD hh:mm:ss**

Let us look at a few examples below.

[root@server ~]# journalctl --since today

[root@server ~]# journalctl --since "2015-04-23 20:30:00" --until "2015-05-23 20:30:00"

There are more fields attached to the log entries, which will be visible only if you use the verbose option by using **verbose** with the journalctl command.

[root@server ~]# journalctl -o verbose

This will print out detailed journalctl entries. The following keywords are important for you to know as a system admin.

- _COMM, which is the name of the command
- _EXE show the executable path for the process
- _PID will show the PID of the process

- _UID will show the user associated with the process
- _SYSTEMD_UNIT show the systemd unit, which started the process

You can combine one or more of these options to get an output from the journalctl command as per your requirement. Let us have a look at the example below, which will print journal entries that contain the systemd unit file sshd.service bearing the PID 1183.

[root@server ~]# journalctl _SYSTEMD_UNIT=sshd.service _PID=1183

Systemd Journal Preservation

In this section, we will learn how to make changes to the **systemd-journald** configuration such that the journal is stored on the disk instead of memory.

Permanently storing the system journal

The system journal is kept at **/run/log/journal** by default, which means that when the system reboots, the entries are cleared. The journal is a new implementation in Red Hat Enterprise Linux 7.

We can be sure that if we create a directory as **/var/log/journal**, the journal entries can be logged there instead. This will give us an advantage that historical data will be available even after a reboot. However, even though we will have a journal that is persistent, we cannot have any data that can be kept forever. There is a log rotation, which is triggered by a journal on a monthly basis. Also, by default, the journal is not allowed to have a dusk accumulation of more than 10% of the file system it occupies, or even leave less than 15% of the file system free. You can change these values as per your needs in the configuration file at **/etc/systemd/journald.conf** and one the process for systemd-journald starts, the new values will come into effect and will be logged.

As discussed previously, the entries of the journal can be made permanent by creating a directory at /var/log/journal

[root@server ~]# mkdir /var/log/journal

You will need to make sure that the owner of the /var/log/journal directory is root and the group owner is systemd-journal, and the directory permission is set to 2755.

[root@server ~]# chown root:systemd-journal /var/log/journal

[root@server ~]# chmod 2755 /var/log/journal

For this to come into effect, you will need to reboot the system or as a root user, send a special signal **USR1** to the systemd-journald process.

[root@server ~]# killall -USR1 systemd-journald

This will make the systemd journal entries permanent even through system reboots, you can now use the command **journalctl -b** to show minimal output as per the latest boot.

[root@server ~]# journalctl -b

If you are investigating an issue related to system crash, you will need to filter out the journal output to show entries only before the system crash happened. That will ideally be the last reboot before the system crash. In such cases, you can combine the **-b** option with a negative number, which will indicate how many reboots to go back to limit the output. For example, to show outputs till the previous boot, you can use **journalctl -b -1**.

Maintaining time accuracy

In this section, we will learn how to make sure that the system time is accurate so that all the event logs that are logged in the log files show accurate timestamps.

Setting the local time zone and clock

If you want to analyze logs across multiple systems, it is important that the clock on all those systems is synchronized. The systems can fetch the correct time from the Internet using the Network Time Protocol NTP. There are publicly available NTP projects on the Internet like the Network pool Project, which will allow a system to fetch the correct time. The other option is to maintain a clock made up of high quality hardware to serve time to all the local systems.

To view the current settings for date and time on a Linux system, you can use the **timedatectl** command. This command will display information such as the current time, the NTP synchronization settings and the time zone.

[root@server ~]# timedatectl

The Red Hat Enterprise Linux 7 maintains a database with known time zones. It can be listed using the following command.

[root@server ~]# timedatectl list-timezones

The names of time zones are based on zoneinfo database that IANA maintains. The naming convention of time zones is based on the ocean or continent. This is followed by the largest city in that time zone or region. For example, if we look at the Mountain Time in the USA, it is represented as "America/Denver".

It is critical to select the correct name of the city because sometimes even regions within the same time zone may maintain different settings for daylight savings. For example, the US mountain state of

Arizona does not have any implementation of daylight savings and therefore falls under the time zone of "America/Phoenix".

The **tzselect** command is used to identify zone info time zone names if they are correct or not. The user will get question prompts about their current location and mostly gives the output for the correct time zone. While suggesting the time zone, it will not automatically make any changes to the current time on the system. Once you know, which timezone, you should be using, you can use the following command to display the same.

[root@server ~]# timedatectl set-timezone America/Phoenix

[root@server ~]# timedatectl

If you wish to change the current date and time for your system, you can use the **set-time** option with the timedatectl command. The time and date can be specified in the format ""YYYY-MM-DD hh:mm:ss". If you just want to set the time, you can omit the date parameters.

[root@server ~]# timedatectl set-time 9:00:00

[root@server ~]# timedatectl

You can use the automatic time synchronization for Network Time Protocol using the **set-ntp** option with the timedatectl command. The argument to be passed along is **true** or **false, which** will turn the feature on or off.

[root@server ~]# timedatectl set-ntp true

The Chronyd Service

The local hardware clock of the system is usually inaccurate. The **chronyd** service is used to keep the local clock on track by synchronizing it with the configured Network Time Protocol NTP servers. If the network is not available it synchronizes the local clock to the RTC clock drift that is calculated and recorded in the **driftfile, which** is maintained in the configuration file at /etc/chrony.conf.

The default behavior of the chronyd service is to use the clocks from the NTP network pool project to synchronize the time and no additional configuration is needed. It is advisable to change the NTP servers if your system happens to be on an isolated network.

There is something known as a **stratum** value, which is reported by an NTP time source. This is what determines the quality of the NTP time source. The stratum value refers to the number of hops required for the system to reach a high performance clock for reference. The source reference clock has a stratum value of 0. An NTP server that is attached to the source clock will have a stratum value of 1, while a system what is trying to synchronize with the NTP server will have a stratum value of 2.

You can use the **/etc/chrony.conf** file to configure two types of time sources, **server** and **peer**. The stratum level of the server is one level above the local NTP server. The stratum level of the peer is the same as that of the local NTP server. You can specify one or more servers and peers in the configuration file, one per line.

For example, if your chronyd service synchronizes with the default NTP servers, you can make changes in the configuration file to change the NTP servers as per your need. Every time you change the source in the configuration file, you will need to restart the service for the change to take effect.

[root@server ~]# systemctl restart chronyd

The chronyd service has another service known as **chronyc, which** is a client to the chronyd service. Once you have set up the NTP synchronization, you may want to know if the system clock synchronizes correctly to the NTP server. You can use the **chronyc sources** command or if you want a more detailed output, you use the command **chronyc sources -v** with the verbose option.

[root@server ~]# chronyc sources –v

CHAPTER 10

Archiving Files

In this system, we will learn how to compress files and archive them. We will also learn to extract the compressed file. We will learn the different compression techniques that are available in Linux and why compression is necessary and how it is useful to make the life a system admin easy.

Managing Compressed Archives

In this section, we will learn about the tar command and how it is used to compress and archive files. We will also learn how to use the tar command to extract data from existing archived files.

What is tar?

Compression and archiving of files is useful for taking backups of data and for transferring huge files from one system to another over a network. The **tar** command can be used to achieve this, which is the most common and one of the oldest methods used to archive and compress files on the Linux system. With the tar command, you can compress an archive using the **gzip, xz,** or **bzip2** compression.

The tar command is accompanied by one of the following three actions.

- **c, which** is used to create an archive
- **t, which** is used to list the content of an archive
- **X, which** is used to extract from an existing archive

The options that are commonly used along with the tar command are as follows.

- **f file name, which** will be the file that you want to use
- **v** stands for verbosity, which shows the list of files getting archived or being extracted

Using tar to archive files and directories

If you are looking to create a tar archive, you need to ensure that there is no existing archive with the same file name as the one that you intend to create because the tar command will not give you any prompt and will overwrite the existing archive file.

You will need to use the **c** option to create a new archive followed by **f file name**.

[root@server ~]# tar cf archive.tar file1 file2 file3

This command will create an archive file named archive.tar, which will contain the files file1, file2, and file3.

Listing contents of a tar file

The **t** and **f** options are used with the tar command to list the contents of a tar file.

[root@server ~]# tar tf /root/etc/etc.tar

etc/

etc/fstab

etc/mtab

...

Using tar to extract an existing archive

The **x** and **f** options are used with the tar command to list the contents of a tar file.

[root@server ~]# tar xf /root/etc/etc.tar

Adding a **p** to the option ensures that all permissions are preserved after extraction

[root@server ~]# tar xpf /root/etc/etc.tar

Creating a compressed tar archive

There are three types of compression techniques that can be used with the tar command. They are as follows.

- **z, which** is used for a gzip compression with filename.tar.gz or filename.tgz extension

- **j** used for bzip2 compression with a filename.tar.bz2 extension

- **J** used for a xz compression with a filename.tar.xz extension

You can pass one of these options with the regular tar create command to get the required compressed archive.

Example: If you wish to create a tar archive with a gzip compression, you can use the following command.

[root@server ~]# tar czf new.tar.gz /etc
This will create a compressed archive of the content of the /etc directory and name it *new.tar.gz*.

Extracting a compressed tar archive

You can use the **x** option with the tar command and pass one of the compression options along with it to extract the contents of a tar archive.

Example: If you wish to extract a tar archive file, which has a gzip compression, you can use the following command.

[root@server ~]# tar xzf /root/etc/etc.tar.gz

This will extract all the contents from the compressed archive at */root/etc/etc.tar.gz* and place all its files in the home directory of the root user since that is the present working directory of the root user.

Conclusion

User data is the most expensive entity in the world today. Compromise in data can result in huge losses for an organization. You can maintain a computer at home with a reasonable amount of security such as a simple antivirus software. However, given the amount of data that is present on business related systems on the Internet, they are more prone to attackers, and therefore, the level of effort to maintain security on business machines is way more than a personal computer. But Linux operating systems have proved to be a secure platform for a choice of the operating system on server systems for big organizations. Given the open-source nature of the Linux operating system development, security patches come faster for Linux than they come out for any other commercial operating systems, making Linux the most ideal platform with respect to security.

All this said and done, what comes into the spotlight is the job profile of a Linux system administrator. There is a huge demand for this profile in all the major organizations worldwide, which work on Linux systems. This book provides a beginner's course to the Linux system and we hope that it will encourage you to learn advanced Linux system administration in the future.

Made in the USA
Las Vegas, NV
14 September 2022